Also by [barcode MW00623110]

Nonfiction

The INFJ Writer:
Cracking the Creative Genius of the World's Rarest Type

Firefly Magic:
Heart Powered Marketing for Highly Sensitive Writers

Fiction

West Coast Trilogy:
Between the Shadow and Lo (Book 1)
West Is San Francisco (Book 2)
Enormous Forces (Book 3)

Firefly Magic

Heart Powered Marketing for Highly Sensitive Writers

Lauren Sapala

VIVIAN BELL
PUBLISHING

Contents

Part Three

Keeping the Magic Alive

Introduction

This is not a normal marketing book.

By "normal," I mean that this isn't a book that will teach you how to monetize your blog, optimize Facebook ads, or launch a killer PR campaign. There are thousands of books focused on those specific marketing topics (and more) already out there. However, in my experience, a lot of writers aren't reading those books. In fact, they tend to avoid them.

The resistance many writers have to learning about marketing is not new information to any of us. For a very long time, business and art have been divided in our society, and in conflict with each other. In recent years that's begun to change. You can find many books and blogs today that teach creative folks how to excel at business. But, in my opinion, not much of this material goes to the root of the problem.

One big truth that feeds this "root" is the fact that most writers have Highly Sensitive temperaments. What I mean by "Highly Sensitive" goes beyond the classic definition of a Highly Sensitive Person: someone who is more physically sensitive than most of the population to sounds, smells, textures, and painful and pleasurable sensations. Instead, I am referring to those people who are more *emotionally, mentally, and spiritually sensitive* than most of the population: those who identify as HSP, but also those who are introverted, intuitive, empathic, and/or identify as an INFJ or INFP personality type.

Over the years, as a writing coach who works exclusively with Highly Sensitive Writers, I have come to see that the writers who fit my definition of Highly Sensitive experience unique challenges when it comes to marketing their work. In the interviews I conducted with Highly Sensitive Writers for this book I heard the same statements again and again. Problems with marketing stemmed from so many writers being introverts, or "not good at business stuff," or feeling sleazy or disconnected around any type of sales work. When I dug below the surface though, I found that every one of these statements led back to an underlying, deeply entrenched belief system that was getting in the way of any real forward motion.

I also realized this is the reason so many of the methods that try to help Highly Sensitive Writers learn about marketing fail. It's not enough to tell a Highly Sensitive Writer she deserves to make money. It doesn't work if you give her examples of how business and art can mix. If a Highly Sensitive Writer is holding a certain ingrained belief system, no amount of evidence that disproves that belief system will be absorbed long term. A few minutes after a person takes in information contrary to existing beliefs, the ego quickly goes about undermining it. And then we're right back to square one.

The only thing that is truly effective when it comes to dismantling limiting beliefs is to give people tools to explore their own minds and their own feelings; a way to shift perspective *on their own*. Working with limiting beliefs is a process of intense personal growth, and personal growth is always highly individual and must be embarked on *by choice*. No exceptions.

So, instead of this being a marketing book that tells you all the ways you can "get better" at marketing and lists dozens of tips and

Introduction

tricks that might be outdated in a few years anyway, this is a book that will give you incredibly powerful thought tools that you can use if (and when) you're interested in changing your own mind about marketing and the way you feel about it.

This is also a different kind of marketing book in that you won't find advice on how to "win the game" or "beat the competition." Like almost all Highly Sensitive Writers, that way of thinking doesn't work for me. Instead, this book will teach you how to use marketing work to access your own inner light, and also how to see and encourage the light in others. It's my belief that each human soul on this planet is like a firefly: We all have the ability to fly, and to glow. We all have the power to light ourselves from within, and to contribute our light to the net of stars we see when many fireflies come together in community on a warm July night. We all have a way to instantly activate this precious inner light: through our heart center, the most incredible source of power in the world.

This is what I call Firefly Magic, and it's the whole idea behind "heart powered marketing." In my opinion, it's also the only way Highly Sensitive Writers will be successful doing any kind of marketing work at all.

Finally, before we begin, I want to remind my readers that there is no right way to do anything. There is only the way that each of us creates as we walk our own unique path.

My hope is that this book gives you a little help along your way.

Part One
Seeing the Magic

Chapter 1

Ambition and Integrity: Not Only Can They Coexist, They Can Actually Be Friends

I decided to write this book because I noticed a pattern related to writers and artists, especially those who identified as Highly Sensitive People. I'm an intuitive personality, introverted and Highly Sensitive myself. So, when I "notice a pattern" I can't let it go. I'm like a dog with a bone. And if the pattern is tied to something that seems to be blocking people from reaching their potential, I become obsessed, fast.

The pattern, in this case, was a resistance to sales and marketing.

As with all patterns, I used my intuition and emotion to feel into it. On one side, there was business. Efficient, rational, productive, and also, a bit cold. On the other side there were the writers. Warm, alive, sometimes gorgeously irrational, and full of poetry and dreams.

How could these two things possibly fit together?

This wasn't the first time I had asked myself this question. Even as a small child, I knew I wanted to be an artist. To me, artists were magic people. I wanted to write poetry and I wanted to create. I wanted to explore my own soul and touch the souls of others.

But as the grownup woman who had, indeed, ended up becoming a writer, I was now in a place where I needed to learn how to market my writing if I ever wanted more than just my friends to read it. So, how would I do that? Would I have to abandon my warm, alive world full of beauty and dreams for the cold sterile efficiency of the business mindset?

The more writers I talked to, the more I knew I wasn't the only one asking this very question.

But before I even started interviewing writers about their feelings on sales and marketing, I had nailed down one thing that I knew to be true: A large proportion of writers share the same temperament. We are Highly Sensitive, emotionally-centered, empathic, intuitive, and deeply connected to the earth and our own hearts. We hold very clear values that seem almost inborn, and that rarely change over the course of our lifetimes: compassion, kindness, curiosity, creativity, and acceptance.

Something inside of us clashes with the whole sales and marketing thing. Or...we *think* something inside of us clashes. We *assume* some part of our values don't fit, and won't ever fit, with the values of the business world.

Maybe, I thought, the conflict lies within our own thoughts. Maybe, just maybe, the real problem is that we have limiting belief systems in place that hold us back from seeing how the two things can not only fit together, but also work toward each other's growth and evolution.

So, I kept asking questions. I was still after that hard kernel of truth in the center of the riddle. Then, after an intense personal marketing experience of my own, I saw it.

The answer is *integrity*.

Highly Sensitive Writers have a highly developed sense of integrity.

Our integrity acts as our internal compass, and without this compass we would be lost in life. We are the people who literally can't sleep at night when we feel we've possibly acted in a way that compromises our own sense of honor.

My hunch was then confirmed when I received answers to a few of the questions about marketing I had sent to the Highly Sensitive People in my writing network.

One memoir writer said:

I've always had retail and sales-type jobs, and I can market and sell someone else's work, easily—but to market my own work feels a bit ego-driven and manipulative. I want to be the artist, not the salesperson.

This was the thorny conflict that Highly Sensitive Writers couldn't get past. How is it possible to be both an artist AND a salesperson? Because aren't most (if not all) salespeople ego-driven and manipulative?

Well, yes, some are. But some really aren't. It depends on the person, just like anything else. But when we enter the realm of limiting beliefs the unconscious mind doesn't slow down long enough to judge anything on an individual basis. It tends to leap ahead and group things based on assumptions, instead.

The assumption about the ego-driven, manipulative salesperson is very prevalent in our culture, so it's an easy leap to make.

Another writer told me this:

Honestly, the people who are really "good at marketing" in the traditional sense [seem to] ... lack a sense of shame. That sounds really harsh, and maybe it's not the right word, but...I don't like feeling hustled and I don't want to hustle people when marketing my book.

Then there are other writers... who send me wonderfully helpful information and manage to market themselves and their services gently, and enrich my life in a non-annoying way. They seem to genuinely want to be helpful, and not just for money. I aspire to that. I can't be shameless, but I know I can be helpful. That's what I'm focused on.

What snagged my attention here was the use of the word "hustle." Since starting up my own business as a writing coach and editor a few years ago, I was always on the lookout for any information about how to improve a "side hustle," which is exactly what my business was. I had read the book *The Hustle Economy* by Jason Oberholtzer and got all fired up to write, inspire, create, and share everything I made with the world. But then I looked for Meetup groups in San Francisco based on that search term, "hustle," and what I got back wasn't pretty.

The very first group I found said that if I wanted to be a member I needed to be "frighteningly ambitious."

Whoa.

Now, I am a writer, so I do pay more attention to words and the way they're used than the average person, but "frighteningly"? Really? Why couldn't I just be ambitious, without the side of frightening? When I thought of "frightening" I thought of Pennywise the clown from Stephen King's terrifying book *IT*. I specifically thought of this scene where Pennywise is all up in a little kid's face with his piercing crazy eyes and huge lion fangs bared, ready to chomp into the kid's throat. Okay, yes, this might be extreme, but I also don't think it was any coincidence that my subconscious mind immediately linked the image of "ruthless predator attacks innocent party" with the vibe I got from this group of people who described themselves as "frighteningly ambitious."

"Frighteningly ambitious" also doesn't seem to point to someone who is interested in being of service to others on a deep level, or in tapping into the profound feeling of interconnectedness between all living beings on the planet. After all, in order to be frightening, you have to be actually *scaring* someone else. Pushing others into an energy of fear doesn't sit well with me, and I know it doesn't sit well with other sensitive intuitive people.

So, maybe the assumptions were true. Maybe salespeople are ego-driven and manipulative, and to do well at marketing one has to be pushy and hustle people.

Except, the way Jason Oberholtzer used the word "hustle" in

The Hustle Economy (having your own creative business and working hard at it) still spoke to me. I knew what I was doing as a writing coach wasn't hustling people. Far from it. But, I was hustling *something*.

I looked a bit more closely at how I worked as a writing coach.

Before every single session with a client, I pray. I don't pray to anyone or anything specific. I just offer up a prayer to the Universe and ask to please be of service to the person I'm about to talk to on the phone. I ask to fully access my gifts and assist them in whatever way possible I can at this time. I ask for help in getting my ego out of the way. I ask for help in knowing when to actively listen, and when to speak with noble truth.

And then I get on the phone with my client and basically shut up for an hour and let them talk.

Maybe I was hustling my own energy. Maybe the thing I was pushing was the opportunity people had with me to find a safe space where they could expand and grow.

Much of the time, during these calls with clients, I am tempted to break in with suggestions for what I think they should do, or observations that I think are really cool. I always get this gentle nudge when I have those urges, this little push that says, "Move back into integrity. This isn't about you." The moment I see that my ego has been trying to angle its way into the conversation and I move back into integrity I feel an immediate calmness envelope me. When I do finally open my mouth, my words are something that the client actually does need to hear.

I had come back to integrity as the answer again.

Integrity was the key difference between hustling energy to build a thriving creative business, and being a "frighteningly ambitious" hustler.

Suddenly, something else made sense, too. Another writer I had interviewed told me this:

*Being effective feels like the hardest part [about marketing].
I'm sure I can overcome my fears and try to market my book, but I*

don't trust my instincts in this area. It seems likely that anything I try will turn out to be ineffective, because the tasks of marketing are not where my strengths lie...My internal compass, which is my trusted companion in matters of the psyche and heart, is almost useless when it comes to practical tasks. I see marketing as one of those tasks.

This Highly Sensitive Writer, like so many others, was afraid that her most valuable gift—her internal compass—had no place in the world of marketing. She assumed that her natural integrity would either be useless, or even make things harder for her, when she tried to market her book.

She went on to say this:

Nothing interests me about [marketing], other than the idea that marketing is something that my book needs if it's going to thrive and find its way. It needs and wants to be out in the world, not stuck in my head or on my computer, so for my book's sake, I'll learn what I need to learn and do what I need to do.

It was clear to me that this writer felt like a loving mother who will sacrifice everything for her child. She'll do work she hates, just to put food on the table and ensure the child is given opportunities to make its way in the world.

But what if this writer understood that she didn't have to abandon her integrity to get really good at marketing? What if she realized that her integrity was actually one of her *best advantages* in the marketing world? What if she knew that her internal compass was *exactly what she needed* to help her find the people who would love to read her book?

A third writer said this when I interviewed him about his marketing fears:

The hardest part of marketing to me would be the feeling that I have to upsell my own work. I don't think I would come across as genuine and keep any integrity in the role of a marketer, in person or online.

There was that word again. Integrity.

What if this writer realized that he could keep his integrity *and* shine in the role of marketer?

It just might change everything.

I thought about examples like Martin Luther King, Jr. and Mother Teresa. They were certainly ambitious, but their ambition wasn't frightening. More like, compassionate. Both were also hustlers in their own way. They hustled for donations, volunteers, and increased social awareness. So, what if "hustling" doesn't have to be manipulative, and instead might symbolize a method of devoted commitment to one's life purpose?

What if an artist and a salesperson could be the *same* person, both operating from a soul-level energy of integrity?

It seems like if we could make that shift in thinking, Highly Sensitive Writers might feel much differently about marketing.

Take some time with these next exercises. It might be helpful to read them now, think them over for the next few days, and then come back to them when you're ready:

Do you have a set of "rules to live by"? Were these rules passed down to you from your parents, did you create them on your own, or is it a mix of the two?

Is there anything you think you might have to do to be "good at marketing" or to market your book that might compromise the rules you live by?

Take a deep breath and center yourself deep in your core. Feel yourself in your body and concentrate your attention on your heart. Imagine your heart actually breathing in and out. Now, cast your mind back to a time when you did something for someone else (it can be a person, an animal, or a plant) that was totally selfless. Feel that feeling in your body now, that light happy feeling of having been of service to someone. That's integrity.

Now, think about a time when you compromised yourself.

Maybe you told a lie, or misrepresented something, or acted with a false persona to impress someone else. Remember that feeling and let it course through your body. You might have a feeling of anxiety, fear, or hiding or feeling small. That's how it feels when you move out of your integrity.

Write a simple statement that will remind you of how to move back into integrity. It might be something like, "Remember the time I saved the kitten up in the tree," or "Dad always said he was proud of my honesty." Whatever it is, it should be personal, and it should immediately give you that gentle nudge to reconnect with your integrity. Hang this up over your writing workstation.

Now, when you go forward with your marketing work, do an integrity check with your body first. Did you just put together your book promo and you're about to blast it out on Twitter? Check in with your body and see how you feel. Are you in integrity? Okay, cool. Blast away. Are you about to put a marketing strategy in place solely because that's what the latest popular article said you should do? Do an integrity check. Does it feel weird and pushy and "not you"? Ok, that's cool too. Let's scrap that idea and move onto something else.

Chapter 2
Feeling Overwhelmed by Marketing? Turn Off Your Rational Brain, Turn On Your Intuition

When I decided to write this book I started my research by interviewing writers. Almost immediately, one particular issue came up again and again in the various answers I received to my questions. Over 75% of writers said their number one problem was the feeling of being over-whelmed, even downright intimidated, by the amount of work that marketing might involve. Not to mention the amount of new knowledge they might have to learn to even get started.

One writer had this to say:

When I think about marketing I feel tired. When I am writing I spend a lot of time within, creating other people and worlds. To me, even though I do write for a specific audience and think about them while writing, it seems like a whole other world to connect with them, and to put my book out there myself...it feels like I would have to completely change my brain's focus...I do feel like I could learn more, it's just overwhelming.

Another writer said this:

[Marketing my book] feels like a big hill to climb. It's hard enough learning how to write my book; marketing feels like an extra skill set that I have to develop, which means time away from

writing. Also, I feel like I'm supposed to have some kind of "message" or theme or brand—and I just don't have that, at least not yet. So, I'm not exactly sure what I'm supposed to be marketing other than the book I'm writing, which is a long way from complete. I'm working on building a small platform, but it's easy to get distracted from it.

Still a third writer told me this:

I really don't believe I belong in the growing and changing landscape of marketing...the thought of self-promotion feels daunting. I'd rather leave the marketing to someone who has developed a passion for it.

Overwhelming, daunting, a "big hill to climb," these are just a few of the words and phrases the writers I interviewed used to describe that feeling of creeping fatigue they experienced whenever they thought about learning new marketing skills.

Of course, I understood how they felt because I've been there myself.

When I released my first novel, *Between the Shadow and Lo*, I nearly gave up on marketing altogether. I had spent weeks researching ways to promote the book and hours googling "best Kindle promotion tactics." My brain was swimming from the glut of information. Some authors said I needed to offer my book for free. Others said free didn't work anymore and I needed to do a 99-cent promotion instead. Some experts said I needed to use Amazon ads, others said Google Adwords was the way to go. Still others told me to look for genre-specific review sites and take out advertisements with them. On top of that I quickly learned about Book Bloggers, Booktubers, and Bookstagrammers and I felt like I needed to have all three on my radar.

After a while of sorting through this massive pile of recommendations and advice, I was done. It was too much. I was overwhelmed, but I was also sorely disappointed. I felt like I hadn't really learned anything useful, and like I had also wasted a lot of energy. I have an extremely busy schedule, so throwing away precious time on useless "research" really impacts my creative life. I was frustrated and annoyed and I just wanted to quit.

That's when I shut down the computer and went for a long walk.

I'm an introvert, and a Highly Sensitive Person. I'm empathic and intuitive, and I take a long time to process things. I'm not a "doer." I'm not one of those people who jumps into the game, gets into the action, or thrives under pressure. I tend to sit on the sidelines for a good long while to observe the game, and then maybe I'll take something I learned by watching and make up my own game with it. My biggest strength, by far, is my intuition. In order for me to take any kind of action, I have to go inward first and look at what's surfacing in my soul.

I realized, during that long walk, that while I was jumping from website to website in an attempt to make quick decisions on the fly about what marketing tactics to use, I was trying to be a "doer." And in the process, I was ignoring my greatest gift: my slow, thoughtful intuition that always puts things together by pieces. Instead of trying to "get in the game" with everyone else, I needed to step back and find the next piece that *felt right to me*, and concentrate on just that piece. I needed to go within and listen to my intuition.

So, how do I know when my intuition is trying to tell me something? Well, it doesn't feel like a big grand announcement from the depths of my soul. And it's not accompanied by trumpets or any loud dinging noises to get me to pay attention. Usually, when my intuition speaks to me it feels more like a gentle nudge. A small push to look at something that's been right in front of my face all along.

In this instance, I thought about all the marketing strategies I had just discovered. Early in my research, I had stumbled across a basic how-to guide on doing a 99-cent Kindle promotion. I remembered now that it had sounded fun to me. It was nearing the end of October and when I read about "Kindle countdown deals" I had immediately thought about how I could do a five-day deal offering my book for 99 cents to celebrate the lead-up to Halloween, one of my favorite holidays. Halloween and October are darker times of the year and my book is pretty dark. Images of my book set up with pumpkins and sparkly purple lights had flashed into my head and gotten me excited.

But then, I had continued pushing the research. Instead of slowing down and letting my natural creativity get playful with the idea that was already calling to me, I had doggedly trudged through reading more articles and more recommendations and absorbing more and more information until I went into complete overload. I had gotten stuck because I had this idea that I needed to have a big fancy marketing campaign and a complicated business strategy to sell my book. Playing around with pumpkins and purple lights had just sounded like too much fun to be serious work.

But now, my intuition was guiding me to slow down and go back to the idea that had called to my playful, creative side. And I knew my intuition was right, it had never let me down. The pumpkins and purple lights were where I needed to be.

When I told my husband about my idea he jumped in to help and we ended up with an amazing set of Halloween photos—my book elegantly placed in between a glittery pumpkin and magical purple lights—for an October 99-cent promotion that did really well. Not only did I make more sales than I expected, but the promotion reminded a few of my writer friends that they hadn't yet posted a review. When I saw the kind words they posted I felt the love of my creative community, and I got a bit of much-needed encouragement, showing me that other people did appreciate my writing.

I also learned an important lesson.

When it comes to marketing our book it's easy to get overwhelmed because we usually hold a certain idea of what marketing "should be" or "should look like." For many of us, when we think of "marketing" and "sales" we think of huge corporate offices and multi-million-dollar ad campaigns. We think of celebrity endorsements and Coca-Cola in 10-foot-high lights splashed across billboards. We've been chased, coaxed, and cajoled by marketing tactics from one company or another our whole lives, and through the years we've only grown more and more jaded by every next over-the-top marketing trick.

But your kind of marketing doesn't have to be that way. You don't have to know everything before you start. You don't have to spend money you don't have. You don't have to have an aggressive ad campaign or social media strategy that aims to reach a million people.

Instead, you can play around with pumpkins and purple lights. You can take a few fun pictures of your book and post them on your Facebook page. There. You just did it. You just marketed your book.

This is why a Highly Sensitive Writer's intuition makes all the difference. Whenever you feel overwhelmed, or intimidated by all the options, take a long walk and listen to that small, still voice within. What is the thing that would be the easiest for you to do at this time? What is the thing that is staring you in the face? What is the thing that seems "too simple" for you to think of it as marketing?

Maybe you realize that you could send out a friendly email to your family and friends, asking them to check out your book, or review it if they've already read it. Maybe you've been thinking about making an Instagram account and posting some pictures of your book because you're proud of the cover design. Maybe you've gotten friendly with the owner of your local indie bookstore and you remember she mentioned that she's always looking for more author events to put on in the store.

Those thoughts that keep popping up in your mind, those little ideas that sound like fun, the tiny *ah-ha!* moments you have in the shower—every one of these things is your intuition at work. It is constantly and carefully putting the pieces together for you. Your intuition is a brilliant observer and a genius mastermind. It only nudges you in directions already confirmed as solid. Your intuition is never going to tell you to take out a second mortgage on your home and sink it all in television advertisements for your book. Instead, it's going to give you one small wise piece at a time to add to the big-picture puzzle.

So slow down and do what you do best. Go within. Listen to what the voice of your intuition is telling you. What's the next piece? It should be something accessible, affordable, and within reach. Concentrate on doing just that one thing. And then do the next thing. Small actions over time add up to big marketing value.

Don't spend too much time with the following exercises. To whatever extent you can, write whatever comes immediately to mind:

If you already have a book out, is there anything you've always wanted to try as a marketing strategy but you've shot the idea down up until now for whatever reason?

If you're about to launch a book, is there anything you've dismissed as a marketing strategy because it's seemed "too simple"?

Is there anything you could do to promote your book that you haven't done because you've talked yourself out of it due to fear?

Can you brainstorm five simple ways you could improve the marketing for your book this month?

Can you brainstorm one thing you could do today to help improve the marketing of your book?

Chapter 3
Shattering the Illusion: The Marketing Fantasy That Can Undermine Writers

I was on the phone with a long-time client and feeling pretty good about things. We had worked for months to get her manuscript into shape and it was time for her to start querying. She had already decided she wanted to go the traditional publishing route and we had used most of our session to discuss drafting the query letter and synopsis. We only had about 15 minutes left and so I jumped into the next logical step of the process.

"You'll probably want to start thinking about marketing too. There are so many different ways you could go—"

"Why would I want to do that?"

My client's tone had gone from peppy and excited to cold and closed. *Weird*, I thought. But I pressed on.

"Well, it's never really too soon to think about learning more about marketing, and there's so much out there to learn—"

"No, no, no." she cut me off. "I don't need to do that. That's why I'm going with a traditional publisher. I want nothing to do with marketing."

I knew better than to argue. The mood had gone sour and we

wrapped up the rest of the session in a perfunctory manner. *Awkward*, I thought to myself.

Then, a few months later I was at a writer's retreat talking to one of my writer friends about her fantasy novel. Her face lit up and her eyes sparkled as she went into detail about all the latest adventures of the heroine of her book. It was awesome to see. She was obviously very passionate about her story and I always find that kind of enthusiasm catching.

"Have you decided how you want to publish?" I asked. When she said she was going with a traditional publisher, I was curious to know how she made her decision. So, I asked her that too.

"Oh, I don't want to deal with marketing," she said quickly.

"Really?" I said. "I think you might have to learn some marketing skills anyway, even if you do go with a traditional publisher…"

"Oh no," she waved a hand and her eyes softened and then glazed over. I could see she was mentally checking out right in front of me. "They take care of all of that," she said dreamily, and then went back to explaining the ending of her story to me.

Hmmm… I thought. *How interesting.* The reactions I got from writers when I brought up marketing seemed to range from resistant to unconscious. And also, why did I keep running across writers who told me that the publisher would do "all the marketing" for them?

Something about both of these experiences felt weird to me, but I couldn't quite put my finger on it.

It was some time after this that I found myself working with a brilliant memoir writer who had been a computer programmer in the 1960s, long before "programmer" was a common job title. I was in absolute awe of this writer. She had not only become a programmer when hardly any women worked in tech at all, but had also learned how to pilot a plane and traveled around the world. Now in her 70s, she was putting all of her amazing memories down on paper. But it was an experience she said she had in college that really snagged my attention. She mentioned that a lot of women at that time went to college specifically to find a husband. This was not a big secret. In fact, back in the late 50s and early 60s, it was *expected* that once a woman in college found a husband she would most likely drop out of school immediately.

The writer said that she wasn't interested in taking that route. She had always wanted to have an interesting career, and live an interesting life, even if she had to face a lot of her fears to do it.

Now, I'm not judging one way or the other on this. I truly believe that everyone gets to live their life according to their own preferences. But I will say that almost every single *writer* I have ever met comes with a built-in streak of independence and chutzpah a mile wide. In my opinion, there are temperaments that do better in a support role and would rather go along on someone else's ride, and then there are temperaments (like my programmer writer client) that won't be satisfied unless they push themselves to live life on their own terms.

Again, almost every single writer I have ever known falls into the latter camp.

That includes the two writers I mentioned at the beginning of this chapter, who were both counting on a publisher to do all their marketing for them.

So, why were writers who I *knew* were exceptionally intelligent, creative, and independent suddenly turning into the women who went to college only to meet a husband whenever the word "marketing" was brought up?

THAT was what I thought was really weird.

I started doing some research.

I started by reading sales books, lots of sales books. I also read books on marketing, entrepreneurship, and building a creative side business. But it wasn't until I read *APE (Author, Publisher, Entrepreneur)* by Guy Kawasaki and Shawn Welch that I discovered what I was looking for.

In *APE*, Kawasaki lays out a fantasy he says most writers have about the traditional publishing route. As I read his description I flashed back to my own illusions: the assumptions I carried when I was a writer just starting out. I remembered how I had felt ten years ago, when I knew almost nothing about publishing or how it worked. When the only thing I did know, in fact, was that I wanted to be a published author more than anything else. Kawasaki's list of things he says most writers expect from a traditional publisher definitely would have hit home for me at that time.

I, too, had assumed that I wouldn't have to do any of my own marketing. I, too, had believed that the publisher would continue to market my book long after the release date. I, too, had thought the publisher would have better contacts than I could ever hope to have, and also perhaps send me on a cross-country book tour, paying my expenses all the way.

It was only when I started coaching writers, and making friends with dozens of writing bloggers and other writers on social media, that I got a peek behind the curtain and my publisher-does-the-marketing fantasy slowly dissolved.

It had just fallen away so gradually that I forgot that I, too, had once suffered from the writer's marketing fantasy about traditional publishers.

It was only when I got that peek behind the curtain—the peek that turned into a good long look—that I saw the truth. I met one writer whose agent had stopped talking to her. He just flat out didn't answer her emails anymore and hadn't had any contact with her for over a year. I talked to another writer who had a pretty decent deal with one of the Big Five publishers and then left to strike out on her own in self-publishing because she was so sick of waiting 18 months to two years between finishing a book and seeing it released. I made friends with a few different writers who spent their evenings and weekends building their online platform brick-by-brick because their agents and publishers let them know they were responsible for this part of the process and they couldn't spare the time or attention to help them with it.

Now, this is not a book about self-publishing versus traditional publishing. That choice is a very personal one for any writer, and each route has its pros and cons, just like anything else. But this *is* a book that aims to clear away the illusions, confusion, and fear that contributes to limiting beliefs that a lot of writers hold about marketing. And one of those huge illusions is that if you go with a traditional publisher you don't have to worry about marketing at all —you don't have to learn any new skills in this department— because the publisher will do everything for you.

Just as those long-ago women who went to college only to find a husband probably found out somewhere along the way that the things we really want in life always demand we take action to get them ourselves, writers suffering from the publisher-as-marketing-savior fantasy will find out that their assumptions are not based in reality.

The truth is: No matter if you go with self-publishing or a traditional publisher, you are going to be very much on your own for a lot of the marketing process.

Okay, so how are you feeling now? Let's do a quick body check-in. For those of you still working to dissolve the fantasy laid out above you might be going into a fear place. Let me just take a moment to reassure you that it is very, very normal to feel fear and anxiety when you start to take responsibility for some of the big things you want out of life. *You want to be a successful author? Then you're going to have to learn how to market. Period.* Some part of your brain might be exhilarated when you read those words, but it's much more likely (especially if you already have resistance to marketing) that a large part of you feels panicked, powerless, and like you couldn't possibly ever be good at this intimidating new thing.

Again, that is very normal. And also, you're not alone. You might not be able to count on a traditional publisher for as much marketing muscle as you were expecting, but you CAN count on your writing community. That's the fun part. Once you decide to face your fear and jump off the high dive into the world of marketing a book, you will be astounded at how many people come out of the woodwork to help you. You will also surprise yourself. You will learn new things and be so good at some of those things that you will then be able to actually help others with those things too.

~

Let's take a more in-depth look at any "marketing fantasies" you might be holding onto. Grab a few sheets of paper and wait until you have 20 minutes of quiet time to answer these questions:

If you are currently unpublished, how do you picture yourself in the future as a published author? Do you see yourself speaking at bookstores or autographing books? Dig a little deeper. In your fantasy, who set up that speaking engagement? Who blasted out the info on social media? Who made sure you're supplied with a fresh new package of Sharpie markers to sign books? In this fantasy, is it you who makes all that happen, or is there an imaginary PR team supporting you at every turn?

Now imagine that your book has been out for quite some time, maybe two or three years. Are people still buying it? Are people still hearing about it? How are they hearing about it and buying it? Who's making that happen, you or someone else?

Picture yourself landing the book deal that dreams are made of. You sign a three-book contract that gives you a hefty advance, enough to quit your day job and write full time. What are your expectations about how things will go after that? Will you maintain your own social media presence, or will your publisher do that for you? What if sales don't go as well as expected? Will you be able to help that in any way through improved marketing or is that all in your publisher's hands?

Sit and read back over your answers. Can you identify areas where you can see you might have been glossing over the realistic details of the marketing/publishing process? Can you see places where you might have assumed you wouldn't have to take responsibility for your book once it's out in the world?

Chapter 4
Getting Real: On Personal Expectations and Professional Authenticity

Starting in 2013 I began an email correspondence with an online entrepreneur who had become one of my idols. When I had initially stumbled across this guy's blog in 2010 it blew my mind. He was the first person to show me how to build an online presence, how to follow your own heart and your own (sometimes crazy radical) ideas, and how to use writing to get it all across to an audience. When I finally worked up the courage to email him a few years later and he actually emailed me back and we began discussing all these ideas, I could hardly believe it.

As we kept up our exchange I discovered that he was actually a completely normal, down-to-earth person. He was a digital nomad, so my chances of ever meeting him were slim, I thought. Until, that is, he moved to San Francisco.

Let's meet up! My friend suggested. *We can talk about everything in person*, he said. *It will be so much fun.*

I panicked. Then I made excuses. I was too busy, there was no time I could make in my schedule right now. It would be better to wait until this or that thing cleared off my calendar.

Finally, two months later, my friend called me on my bullshit. *Where are you?* he said in an email. *Why haven't we met up?*

I had no choice but to come clean.

I'm too scared, I wrote back. *I know that's weird, but it's the truth. The thought of meeting you in person totally freaks me out.*

At the same time this all went down I was also deep into researching how to improve Kindle sales. Partly to write this book, but also partly to increase sales of my own memoir of alcoholism, *Between the Shadow and Lo.* I was reading articles on how to do 99-cent promotions, and articles on how to best use the five free days the Kindle Select Program gives each author in every 90-day period. I went over a list of over 200 services that offered paid Kindle promotion through email newsletters, and I read accounts from other authors of how they successfully launched or promoted their books and got 700, 1,000, and 3,000 downloads on each campaign day.

Weirdly enough, as I did my Kindle sales research, I was getting that same sinking feeling in my stomach I got whenever I thought about meeting my online friend.

So, as I often do when I'm experiencing a swirl of unpleasant emotions, I sat myself down and probed inside, poking at all the sore spots.

This is NEVER comfortable. But it always gives me some answers.

And, answers I got.

The very first thing I saw was that I was just plain terrified of not being good enough, in both instances. My ego was bringing all its judgmental, fear-based, materialistically-focused energy to the table (as it always does, thanks ego). Not only was my ego making a huge amount of assumptions about what I "should be" in order to "win" either situation, but my ego had also already decided that I was definitely NOT any of those things, and so would most probably "lose" everything I had hoped for.

Again, thanks ego. Super helpful of you, always appreciate your input.

One of the most unhelpful assumptions my ego had made was

that I needed to meet the very specific expectations of my online friend, and the entire Amazon Kindle audience, in order to be accepted by either one. In the case of my friend, my ego told me that I wasn't smart enough or interesting enough, I needed to lose a few pounds, and also, I was too weird. (No matter what the situation, my ego likes to throw in the "too weird" card.) In the case of the Kindle promotion, my ego looked at all the high numbers of downloads everyone else was reporting and told me I should just give up before I even tried. There was no way I would reach 700, 1,000, 3,000—whatever numbers were quoted that I was reading about. No way. So, there was no point in even trying.

This is an emotional issue that everyone struggles with: The fear of being inadequate in some fundamental way and, consequently, unlovable. But it's rarely talked about when we have the conversation on what it means to do marketing work as a writer. Most of the time the dry and rational system of sales knowledge is what we're referencing when we talk about "marketing our book." We hardly ever dig deeper and talk about the underlying emotions that we experience when we compare ourselves to the "others" who are selling books, or the "others" who might potentially read ours, and then judge us for it.

But these complex, and oftentimes conflicting, emotions are the very thing that can hold us back from even attempting to do any marketing work at all.

Just as I decided to run the risk of *never* meeting my friend in person, if only to protect my fragile ego and all its spurious assumptions, many writers make the decision to never promote their work, in order to protect themselves in exactly the same way.

The way to dissolve this tension is to consciously shift away from assumption and into clarity. For instance, in the case of my friend, I had no actual evidence that I needed to have a high IQ or weigh a particular amount for him to accept me as a person. And in fact, if I had met with him and been rejected and then later found out that he didn't want to be friends with me anymore because I didn't meet his intelligence or size standards, I would truthfully have thought that was a bit shallow of him (after I got over the initial sting of it, of course) and a reasonably telling indicator that we weren't all that compatible as people anyway.

In the case of my worrying about whether enough people would download my book, I paused and asked myself a few questions. Did I really want thousands of people to download my book? On the surface, it sure seemed like a good thing, but if I looked closer, was it really? I had only just started to get used to my existing small circle of readers commenting on this or that deeply intimate section of the book. I had only just started to feel that I was resilient enough to be *this* vulnerable with the world. Was a random 3,000-person sampling of the general population reading my book really in the best interest of my own growth and evolution? Some part of me felt excited at the thought, but another, larger part of me felt deeply *not ready*. In my fluttery fear state that my book wouldn't be "enough" I hadn't even noticed that this part of me existed, or that it was begging for me to honor it.

The more questions I asked—and the more I honestly examined what I truly wanted and what was best for me at *this* time in *my* journey—the more I discovered that the answers to those questions were unique to me and my book. No number of articles about what I "should do" or what the marketing process "should look like" were going to be as helpful as listening to my own inner truth.

A week or so later I had the same realization as I was reading the blog of a very successful mystery/suspense author who frequently wrote about the best ways to promote books. This guy was hardcore. He talked about driving across the country and visiting hundreds of small bookstores to meet the booksellers, give out swag, and do impromptu readings. He also said he tried to go to as many conferences a year as he could, and get on as many panels as possible. He advised all his fellow authors to do the same. My heart just sank. This sounded completely overwhelming, not to mention that it wasn't really an option for me at all. I had a two-year-old son at home and a full-time day job. There was no way I could spend months driving around the country promoting my book.

But then, this author shared his two biggest goals: to get on the New York Times Bestseller List and to get noticed by Hollywood and have his books made into blockbuster movies.

Whoa...okay, I thought. Time to take a step back. What were MY goals?

This is where it got a bit interesting. Because getting on the New York Times Bestseller List actually wasn't important to me at all. The kind of stuff I write doesn't have a large audience, it never has and it probably never will. On the fiction side I write dark, transgressive, downright weird stories, and on the nonfiction side I write self-help books for intuitive introverts, who are a small section of the population. The audiences who pack theaters to watch the newest blockbuster movies, and the people who pick the next book they want to read primarily from the NY Times Bestseller List are not usually in my audience. I already knew that and I was already fine with it.

Once I clearly saw that my goals were radically different from mystery/suspense guy's goals, my heart stopped sinking. I wasn't doing it wrong and he wasn't doing it wrong. We just wanted different things. The only reason it took me so long to notice that was because my pesky ego got in the way, yet again.

When we examine ourselves—our unique desires, hopes and dreams, and our unique fears, limitations and realities—we get clarity on what it is we truly want from the experience of writing and publishing books. In my case, I wanted total no-holds barred self-expression in my fictional work. I wanted to express all of the dark, twisted weirdness that is so much a part of me, and all the conflict that comes along with that. In my nonfiction work, I wanted to be of service to other people like me: the Highly Sensitive Writers who have always struggled with self-acceptance, and with finding their place in the world.

And, I really don't care if I ever make the New York Times Bestseller List.

In order to market your work effectively, you have to know what it is that *you* want. If you genuinely do want to make the NY Times Bestseller List, or have one of your books picked up for a movie deal, then own that. That's your dream and the kind of marketing work you do needs to be geared toward making that come true.

But if you're more interested in helping a small group of people who gravitate toward a specialized niche, then it's up to you to pour whatever energy you can in that direction. Maybe you want to do both things—go big and go small—and that's okay too. You can want different things and be effective in marketing with an eye to achieving those different aims, as long as you have clarity about what you want, and what you're planning to do about it.

Take some time to answer these questions as truthfully as you can to dig deeper into your own expectations and goals for marketing your book:

How comfortable are you with the idea of "being famous"? If you were a writer who was as famous as Stephen King, how do you think you would handle it?

Is the goal of your book to earn money for you? Is the goal of your book to be of service in some way? Is it both? How much do you feel you can compromise on the money piece? How much do you feel you can compromise on the service piece?

Do your characters (or the themes in your book) speak to any certain segment of the population? Do they speak to problems or issues that you've gone through in your own life? How important is it to you to help others who have gone through those same issues?

Are you able to express yourself in your writing (whether fiction or nonfiction) in a way that you can't express yourself in real life? How important is it to you that you share the self-expression of your writing with others?

Chapter 5
How You Feel about Money =
How You Feel about Marketing

I grew up in a family with money. My dad was a surgeon and so was my grandfather. We lived in a small town where the cost of living was low, so money stretched a bit further. I lived in a big house and so did my grandparents, they even had a pool. They also drove fancy cars. It was known around town that my family was "rich," but this didn't make me popular. In fact, it seemed to have the opposite effect.

My dad and his parents very strongly identified with having money. They were achievement oriented and disconnected from their emotions. In my family, being number one, having the best car, the most impressive paintings on your living room walls, and money to spare, was seen as the thing to do in life.

But, there was also this other side to my family. It was a side that no one talked about but that I picked up on all the same. My grandfather's parents had been Polish immigrants, settling in Detroit shortly before World War One. They had five kids and they were very, very poor. My grandfather had to work extremely hard to become a doctor. And for many years he made house calls to other immigrants in the poverty-stricken areas of Detroit for little or no fee.

Shortly before my dad died, I happened across his old medical school yearbook. I flipped through the pages, looking at all the different clubs and groups the students joined. I looked for my dad's face and was shocked to find him in a photograph with the "Young Idealists of Tomorrow." The club's description said they were a group of medical students dedicated to serving those who were impoverished and in need.

My dad had also been involved in the peace marches of the 1960s and passionate about improving society so that everyone could receive a fair share. Even though he desperately strove to make more and more money, he also gave most of it away whenever he had it.

Having money is good.

Having money while others have nothing isn't fair.

Luxury items are something to strive for.

Wealth feels uncomfortable and should be disposed of quickly.

As a child and an adolescent, I had no idea I was being imprinted with ideas that conflicted with each other in a very extreme and deeply emotional way. As any other young human does, I just watched my family, day in and day out, and I unconsciously absorbed everything they handed down to me.

These conflicting feelings swirling around inside me came raging to the surface when I hit my adult years. I had this weird problem: I attracted money quickly but then I lost it just as fast. Wherever I worked, people loved me and I did very well, except I was never happy and always ended up feeling like a workaholic doormat. I allowed myself very little, but I still managed to pile up debt. I was totally controlled by this weird mix of "yes-no/good-bad" when it came to money.

It took me until I was 36 years old to realize I needed to do some serious inner work.

That was when I began to examine my past with money, and the patterns around wealth and abundance that had been handed down in my family. I saw that my grandfather and my dad had been so concerned with wealth because they actually wanted *approval.* I also saw that both of them were born healers. Then I looked at my mother's side of the family. My mom had grown up in a very wealthy neighborhood (Grosse Pointe, Michigan) during the 1950s and had been deeply disappointed and hurt by the racism and segregation she observed going on around her. When the 1960s exploded she was more than ready. She left Grosse Pointe forever and moved to Ann Arbor to go to the University of Michigan. Afterwards she and my father moved to our little town, a place that had much less wealth but way more racial integration. She also had the "yes-no/good-bad" conflict going on around money.

And she also passed that down to me.

A lot of stuff started to make sense. Not just stuff about my finances, but also stuff about my feelings around achievement and success.

A few months after I started doing this money work I released my first book, *The INFJ Writer.* I observed myself during the process and what I saw was interesting—and a bit embarrassing. I pushed the "publish" button on Amazon and then…I did nothing. I didn't tell one single person. Not online and not in real life. I just sat there.

After a few days went by I told two of my very close friends. A day or two after that I posted about it on my blog and mentioned it on Facebook. That was it. I didn't do a book launch. I didn't pay for any Kindle marketing. I didn't seek out reviews.

Six months later I put out the print copy and finally started to get rolling on a little bit of marketing. I started reaching out to people on social media and talking about it. I joined some Facebook groups and explored paid advertising. Little by little, I was getting there.

But it was a long, slow process. The same exact stuff that I had unearthed around my money problems came up again around marketing this book. Why? How was money tied into my feelings about marketing my book?

Well, it was quite simple actually. The way that I felt about money and marketing was the same as I felt about abundance.

Specifically, I didn't think I deserved to have wealth, in any way. I felt guilty when I had it. I felt like me having more of something meant that other people had less. I thought that wealth made people arrogant and divided them from their emotions and their true selves. And I didn't feel comfortable with too much attention on me or my accomplishments either. I thought that also made me a bad person in some nebulous, but still very definite way.

This was why marketing my book was so incredibly difficult for me. Why I felt so much resistance, dragged my feet, and did none of the things that could have helped me in the beginning. I partially tried to make my book a success, but I also partially self-sabotaged the whole process so I wouldn't have to deal with anything good that came my way as the result of a successful book.

If you are having problems feeling good about marketing, if you're experiencing a lot of resistance whenever the topic of marketing comes up, it is essential that you begin to look at your attitudes toward money, wealth, and abundance. And just to clarify: money and wealth are not the same thing. Money is money. It's the pieces of paper you trade for stuff, the green bills that come from the bank. Wealth can take many forms, like those fancy cars and paintings my grandparents had, or even a rich community of creatives surrounding you. Wealth can be tangible or intangible, but no matter what form it takes it always has great potential to be of benefit to you in some way.

If you had parents like I did, who held deeply conflicting beliefs about money, wealth, and abundance, there is a very high chance they passed those beliefs down to you. If you grew up rich, you might feel guilty whenever money comes your way. If you grew up poor, you might feel intimidated and think that inviting wealth into your life might also invite a lot of responsibilities you're not prepared to deal with. If you grew up with parents who always told you that you were "getting too big for your britches" you might feel that having a successful book will disconnect you even more from their approval and love. If your parents drove you to always be the best at everything no matter what, you might feel like your book has to be a New York Times Bestseller or else it's just going to be an embarrassment to you.

No matter who you are, or how you were raised, if you're a Highly Sensitive Writer, the chances are high that you're carrying imprinting from the past that strongly affects how you feel and how you act about marketing your book in the present.

All of us have baggage. It's unavoidable. But the process of empowerment starts happening when we look at that baggage and become *conscious* of it. I definitely still have issues around money, wealth, and abundance. They didn't all just magically disappear because I started reading and journaling about this stuff. But now, when those issues crop up, I'm able to recognize what's going on much more quickly and see that I'm engaging in resistance, or self-sabotage, or procrastination because I'm afraid. Something has triggered some old outdated belief system that I'm still lugging around and my mind is desperately trying to get back to feeling secure, and "security" to the ego always means not challenging the old belief system.

Now, when I launch a book I hit the "publish" button, post about it on my blog, Facebook, and Twitter, send out an email newsletter, and hit up my list of writer friends for help with promotion, reviews, and plain old encouragement.

Now, I don't need to stay invisible, because I'm okay with being uncomfortable.

∼

After you do these exercises, be prepared for memories, revelations, and epiphanies to surface long after you've done the written work. Whatever emotions come up, receive them without judgment. If you do find judgment coming up, remind yourself that these are just observations you're making and try to shift back into neutral:

How does/did your father feel about money and wealth?

How does/did your mother feel about money and wealth?

How would your family members react if you made a lot of money from one of your books?

What kind of jobs have you held in your life? Have you always felt comfortable asking for a promotion or a raise, or not at all?

What kind of jobs have your parents held? How did they feel about those jobs?

If you're self-employed, how did you decide on your rates? How does raising your rates make you feel?

A lot of people like to imagine what they would do if they won the lottery. I'd like you to imagine instead that you won $10,000. What would you do with it? Would it be gone quickly or would you be able to hold onto some of it? What does it feel like when you imagine that $10,000 being spent?

How do you feel about spending the money you have now? Do you hold onto money as long as possible and deny yourself little luxuries? Or does money run out of your wallet like water?

How do you feel about incredible amounts of abundance (money, love, good food, a beautiful house)? Do you think you deserve it?

Chapter 6
Selling Ourselves: How Our Inner Prostitute Hurts and Heals Us

In the fall of 2007 I started a dream job. Within a few months it quickly became a nightmare.

I was working for a glamorous startup company that offered media services to published authors. We were very exclusive and had more than a few famous names on our client list. I had spent more than a year and a half trying to get this job. The CEO was someone I idolized. From the moment I heard the company was being launched I wanted nothing else than to be a part of it.

But, within a month of working at this place, I realized I had made one of the biggest mistakes of my life.

Or, that was how I felt at the time. I didn't yet understand all the lessons I would learn from that job. I didn't yet know that the experience would furnish me with the material for my second novel. I only knew that I had somehow badly misjudged my boss's character. Instead of being a guardian angel, my boss was a ruthless narcissist.

Every psychological issue I had involving disempowerment, exploitation, and day-to-day survival came up for review.

I went to work every day with knots in my stomach and a

migraine already faintly throbbing through my skull. I had to spend nine or more hours at the office (workaholism was a requirement for the job) and every minute felt like torture. The company culture repulsed me. The things I saw other employees going through made me feel ill. The worst part was that I knew if I continued to stay at that job I was contributing to the dysfunction.

But…I didn't quit.

It took me eight months of fighting myself—kicking, screaming, and having a full-on freak-out the entire time—before I left. Eight months doesn't sound like a long time, but when you're a sensitive intuitive person in a situation unfolding in direct opposition to your moral compass it feels like about a thousand years.

For me, at that time, this experience wasn't just about a toxic job. And it wasn't entirely about the poisonous relationship I had with my boss either. It went deeper than that. My role in that dysfunctional company was about me exploring my inner Prostitute, an archetype all of us carry but that only comes out in reaction to certain forms of stress.

Probably the most well-known explanation of the Prostitute archetype comes from Caroline Myss, author of *Anatomy of the Spirit* and *Sacred Contracts* (two of my favorite books and both well worth reading). Myss asserts that although all of us carry a different collection of archetypes, each of us also work with four of the same archetypes throughout our lifetime. These permanent four become activated during times of stress: the Child, the Saboteur, the Victim, and the Prostitute.

According to Myss: "The Prostitute Archetype engages lessons in the sale or negotiation of one's integrity or spirit due to fears of physical survival or for financial gain." This described perfectly the issue I was having with my nightmare job. I didn't have any savings to fall back on, and I also didn't want to lose face with my friends and family, who all knew that I had just landed my "dream job." I didn't want to burn any bridges in the writing community either. Not only did I feel powerless in the present, but I didn't see how I could possibly take any of my own power back in the future either.

That's why it took me eight long months to figure out that no one else had power over me. I decided what and who I gave my power to...and I could *always* take that power back.

Usually, Highly Sensitive People, empaths, and intuitives have a history of giving our power away. Many of us have grown up in toxic homes or with parents who had ongoing conflict with each other or our siblings. Many of us cultivated the persona of the "good kid" or the "quiet one" to avoid being seen. We became very adept at drawing this invisibility cloak over ourselves whenever the energy in a room turned negative. Or, we did whatever needed to be done to make everyone happy, whether that meant glossing over the issue for a little while or slapping a Band-Aid on a festering wound.

Because when our highly sensitive nervous systems are triggered by conflict, the sensation can be so intense that it honestly does feel like a matter of physical survival.

When sensitive intuitive people are exposed to toxic, negative energy our nervous systems get hit hard. It can feel like someone physically punched us in the gut. Being around this kind of dark energy on a constant basis can make us physically ill. We instinctively know this, even if the culture we live in doesn't acknowledge it. So, from a young age, we become very good at jumping in to "fix" the situation, even when it's not ours to fix. Or, we suppress our own needs and withdraw into invisibility. Either way we play it, we are not in integrity. We are not expressing our true feelings or using our real voices. Instead, we're selling ourselves out.

Since sensitive intuitive people are more likely to have this kind of history of being the "fixer" or the invisible one in an attempt to survive a toxic family environment, I think we're also more likely to see the Prostitute archetype wake up whenever we're threatened by financial instability. I also believe that our inner Prostitute comes out whenever we experience emotional instability, which is so intense for us that much of the time we feel it as a physical issue.

This whole drama with the Prostitute archetype is so important for Highly Sensitive Writers to address because it is very likely that it will come up during the marketing process. You might be offered an opportunity that is out of alignment with your integrity, but that promises big bucks. Or, you might end up in a situation that is supposed to be a marketing partnership, but that feels more like you're the one being used. It can go the other way too. You might do a favor for someone and then feel like they "owe" you and they need to "repay" you in some way in order for you to feel emotionally okay with them. All these situations are examples of the Prostitute archetype showing us an issue we need to work with.

And make no mistake, the Prostitute always shows up to teach us something. This is not a "bad" archetype in your psyche. As Myss explains, there are no bad archetypes. Each archetype is neutral and every archetype shows up to reveal something of importance to us. Your inner Prostitute appears whenever it's time to activate your personal power and will support you as you learn how to say "yes" when you mean yes, and "no" when you mean no. Our inner Prostitute gently moves us back into alignment with our integrity whenever we feel like we might have fallen out of balance.

So, for example, imagine that you've just signed up for an online marketing seminar. It looked promising until the company tried to upsell you on a package at checkout, claiming they would give you thousands of email addresses to add to your newsletter list. The deal feels spammy to you. After all, you always get upset when you feel someone might have shared or sold your email address without your permission. But then the voice of fear kicks in, warning that if you don't compromise your values, your book will never sell. When you think about taking the deal you feel powerless, confused, and a little sleazy. This is when you know your inner Prostitute has shown up, and it's here to bring you back into balance with your core values. So, you say no to the deal and then consciously redirect your attention into other marketing options that feel more in alignment with your integrity.

Sometimes, our inner Prostitute is triggered when there is nothing to be triggered about. So, let's go back to the example above. You sign up for the online marketing course and during the checkout process they offer an option to advertise through their newsletter for ten dollars extra. If your Prostitute is triggered at this time, you might become fearful about "selling out" and have an extreme reaction. You might decide these people are only out to get your money or that you're selling out as an artist if you pay for the advertising. You feel sleazy when there is really nothing to feel sleazy about. Because you're so worried about selling out, you back out of the seminar altogether, losing the chance to gain valuable marketing knowledge.

Being conscious about recognizing your inner Prostitute when it makes an appearance makes all the difference. When you're conscious you can clearly discern why you're feeling triggered and what those feelings mean.

In my case, my inner Prostitute was first activated by the job that was so out of whack with my value system, but I was already long overdue for learning how to take back my power. And for many years after that I was distrustful and suspicious of anything that mixed business and writing. It took me a long time to realize my inner Prostitute didn't want to hurt me, she just wanted to help me grow stronger.

$$\sim$$

You don't have to wait years to find out how your inner Prostitute can help you move back into balance around issues of money and power. Try the exercises below to find out how your Prostitute archetype has come into play during your life:

When you were a child, did you ever take on the role of mediator or "peacemaker" in your household? Who were the parties you had to make peace between? Did you ever have to compromise your own needs to make this happen?

When you were a child, did you ever adopt a certain persona to help you "get along"? Were you the "good kid," the "quiet kid," the one "everyone likes"? Did you ever suppress your real feelings in order to gain approval?

In your current life, how much of the time do you make the needs of others a priority over your own needs?

Do you feel threatened or "weird" in any way when you think about paying for advertising for your book?

Are you worried that if you really immerse yourself in marketing and selling your work, that you'll lose touch with the deeper reasons behind your writing?

Do you judge others for "selling out"? What constitutes "selling out" to you?

Chapter 7
Rejection: Digging up the Root of Our Marketing Fears

When I was 22 I went through a bad breakup. It was also a weird breakup because it felt like we weren't ever actually together. I had met the guy my junior year of college and then he almost immediately graduated and moved to Seattle. I followed him there a year later, where we were together for about three months and then he broke things off.

Then I pretty much lost my mind.

I had already been drinking heavily when we broke up, but afterward things got even worse. I did horrible, embarrassing things whenever I ran into him. I tried to fight his new girlfriend. I called him drunk in the middle of the night, almost every night. I threw myself at him and then pointedly ignored him and then did it all over again.

It was an extremely messed up time in my life. So messed up, in fact, that I ended up writing all about it in my first novel, *Between the Shadow and Lo*. I did so many insane humiliating things during those alcoholic years that, as a writer, something in me perversely demanded that I write them all down and share them with the world.

But back to the guy.

The whole time that I was in the middle of losing my mind, becoming a blackout drunk, and doing tons of horrible, embarrassing things, I knew that the way I was reacting was blown out of all proportion. A guy had broken up with me and I had somehow become this exaggerated crazy version of a woman scorned, almost like a comically bad character in a movie. And the thing that kept nudging me at the back of my mind—the knowledge that kept elbowing me in the ribs, urging me to sit up, open my eyes, and pay attention—was that whatever I was going through had nothing at all to do with the guy who dumped me.

Instead, it was tied to a load of ancient emotional baggage.

When the guy left, I felt abandoned. When I felt abandoned, I decided I had been rejected. And when I decided I had been rejected, all hell broke loose.

Like every human being on the face of this planet, I had grown up with a healthy serving of intense emotional experiences, some good and some downright awful. My particular human story included a father who was absent a lot of the time, both physically and emotionally, and a family that dissolved due to death and divorce, and loss and trauma.

I had arrived at the age of 22 years old with not much in the way of emotional coping skills. And, contrary to much of the popular advice out there, I couldn't just "be in the present moment" with this situation. I had no earthly clue how to "breathe through it" or "accept myself" or "stop wishing for things to be different." I was extremely sensitive, emotionally injured, and full of rage and other repressed issues.

In the years since I've done a lot of work and I've resolved a lot of stuff. But occasionally, I still catch myself avoiding certain things, or self-sabotaging carefully laid plans, in order to avoid being rejected.

I still face rejection itself. And then all of that ancient emotional baggage rears its ugly head again.

When I decided to write a book on marketing I knew I wanted

to include a chapter on rejection, and I knew it couldn't be a happy, cheerful chapter. Instead, I wanted to include a chapter that explores rejection just as it really feels. When rejection hits it isn't easy to get over it. It's not a matter of realizing what a great personal growth experience it is, or sifting through the feedback to get those valuable insights that will help you improve your game in the future. Yes, there are those opportunities to be found in rejection, but that doesn't change the way it *emotionally feels* when it happens (totally shitty) or the unconscious avoidance strategies we all employ to get around the aftermath of that feeling (like deciding to never try anything new again because everything now sucks forever).

As you market your book, you will experience rejection. This is a truth that cannot be avoided or made into a cheerful learning experience. The more people who read your book, the more chances there are that you'll get a less than flattering review. The more times you take a chance on paying for advertising, the more likely it is that you'll see some of those dollars wasted. The more you ask people if they might be interested in your story, the more you will sometimes hear nothing but crickets.

This is a law of the universe. The more you do *anything*, the more you will get *all* the results, desired or undesired.

In my marketing interviews with writers, the fear of rejection made a strong showing. One writer said:

I feel vaguely fearful about taking a risk: What if my book is awful and no one wants to read it? What if promoting my book turns out to be an embarrassing mistake?

Another writer said:

Emotionally I'm intimidated by putting my soul out there and being subjected to rejection.

A third writer said:

The thought of marketing is personally frightening to me. I think I have a fear of self-promotion.

These three writers are all saying the same thing in different forms. Not surprisingly, it also sounds a lot like the reasons I gave for not taking a chance on a relationship in the years after my bad breakup. It all basically boils down to: *What if I totally suck? What if no one loves me? What if I'm actually unlovable?*

That last question, especially, is a big gnarly one that needs attention.

In our current culture, there is no end to the snappy, succinct articles online that show you "5 Ways to Love Yourself" or "How Not to Care What Other People Think." Those types of articles might be great for a quick boost, but to do the really effective deep work that will help us stop avoiding and self-sabotaging our best efforts, it's going to take more than a few slick articles. We're going to have to go to the root.

When I was drowning in alcohol and sorrow, reeling from my bad breakup, a very wise deep part of me knew that it wasn't about the guy. But it wasn't until I turned within and faced what it was *really about* that I could begin to move past it. It wasn't until I went back to the root, until I looked at how I felt about my mom and my dad and everything that had gone down in our extremely messed up family situation that I started to get stronger and not so afraid of all my shit getting triggered by possibly being rejected.

So, I did all this inner work, and I started a blog, and finally I was *putting myself out there*. I was *really doing it*. I was *going for the gold*. I was confident, excited, and happy about my progress. I thought, "Yeah, I finally have this fear of rejection thing under control."

Of course, that's when the Universe swooped in and knocked over my house of cards, and then stood smiling and waiting for me to try to pick them all back up again.

I had also finally finished my memoir, which had taken me 11 years to write and morphed into a novel I was calling "autobiographical fiction." It was time to publish the damn thing and I was so scared about it I felt almost dizzy and sick with the knowledge that it was going to be on Amazon and anyone in the whole world could read it.

I felt exactly the way this writer said she felt about marketing when I interviewed her:

The book I'm writing is a memoir, so it's like begging people to read my dirty secrets, which feels weird.

I also felt the way this writer described her marketing fears:

I'm fearful about exposing something that's meaningful to me: What if people read my book and project untrue things onto me? Or what if they read my book and have true insights about me?

Now, not everyone is writing a memoir, but any writer might experience these same fears. Highly Sensitive Writers are people with deep, thoughtful, and emotionally expressive temperaments, so most of what we produce comes directly from our hearts and souls. We're not the type of writer who has researched the top sellers on Amazon and rationally put together a book that speaks directly to a market demand. We're the type of writer who spends years agonizing over a first draft, pulling it piece by bloody piece out of our heads, wavering wildly between wanting to distribute it to the world and then wanting to toss it all into a bonfire. So, whatever we're working on, it means something to us. It is a piece of us, and if people don't like it, or leave a bad review about it, or even just don't say anything at all, this strongly affects us.

It will, more likely than not, bring up all our rejection issues.

The only way to start dissolving the blocks around marketing that are linked to a fear of rejection is to do what I discovered I had to do after that bad breakup. We have to go back to the root. We have to turn inward and look directly into our own darkness. We have to resolve to see whatever it is that wants us to see it, no matter how uncomfortable that might be.

Only then, can we begin to move forward.

The following exercises might bring up emotionally intense material from your past. Go slow and be gentle with yourself. Set the intention to be compassionate and kind toward yourself as you're going through this old baggage. If you feel self-judgment coming on strongly, take a break, get some fresh air and come back to them later:

When you think about being rejected (in any way), what are you most afraid of?

What is your earliest memory of being rejected? Can you name the specific emotions you felt in that experience?

What decision did you make as a result of that early rejection? Did you come up with a coping strategy at that time that you might still use today?

One of the writers I talked to said this during our interview:

The idea of marketing also brings up echoes of an old coping strategy: If I don't try, I won't fail, so I need to find reasons not to try. A fine reason not to try would be, "I hate/can't do marketing."

Do you agree with the above statement or disagree? When you think about your writing and putting it out into the world (which is a form of marketing all by itself) can you see any times when you've found "reasons not to try"?

Think about the most painful aspects of being rejected. Now imagine someone you trust and love—a cherished parent, a wonderful mentor, or even the image of a Goddess you have always connected with—and imagine that person holding you close and comforting you. Imagine them putting their hands on your heart and soothing those burning painful emotions until your heart feels cool (literally) and calm again. Imagine carrying this feeling with you as you move forward in marketing your work and calling upon it for strength whenever you experience rejection.

Chapter 8
From Lone Wolf to Caring Connection: How Shifting Our Mindset Changes Everything

R ight after I graduated from college in Michigan I moved to Seattle. I knew one person there, took a couple of friends along with me, and decided I would figure everything out as it unfolded. About a year later I was working in a little used bookstore during the daytime and drinking my nights away in the city's seedier bars. I was somewhat okay with my new life. I was 22 years old and just as I had planned, I was "figuring it out."

However, every week or so I talked to my friends back home. After college, everyone I had known scattered to the four winds, but I got regular updates on what people were doing. Some people were preparing to take the GRE exams so they could get into graduate school. Others were entering medical or law school. Some of my old friends had landed juicy internships and were now, supposedly, climbing their way up the glittering gold ladder of business success in America.

Hmmm...what was I doing with *my* life?

I pondered this question, and the various paths of my old college friends, as I trundled up and down the quiet aisles of the bookstore and shelved volumes of poetry, histories of World War

II, and psychology and self-help books, all of which never made it onto the shelves without me leafing through at least a few pages. Working at the bookstore wasn't demanding, and I made very little money. It also wasn't what I thought of as "impressive." I wasn't training to be a doctor or a lawyer, or get my PhD. I wasn't engaged in a job that was mostly grunt work now, with the promise of a large income later.

On top of this, the other half of my life was spent in the dirtiest of dive bars, or the craziest of all night clubs. That wasn't really something to boast about either.

So, whenever I compared my life to the lives of my peers, I started to feel pretty bad about things. My achievements seemed paltry, dare I say non-existent, next to those of my old college friends.

But still, somewhere deep down inside, I felt like what I was doing was right. I had this intuition that I was exactly where I needed to be, and that I was getting something out of all these weird Seattle experiences.

Flash forward five years later and I had, suddenly, gotten sober. I was reading the AA Big Book and doing the twelve steps and *shifting* all over the place. I was going through a transformation physically, mentally, emotionally, and spiritually. Up until I got sober, I had continued on that course I was following in Seattle, working in the bookstore by day and partying all night. And from time to time I continued to compare myself to my old classmates and still feel "pretty bad" when I came up short. But then after I stopped drinking and had my transformation it seemed like everything was different. Or, like I was looking at the world through different eyes.

After I got sober I had a spiritual awakening. Simply put, I shifted out of feeling totally alone, isolated, and separate from everyone else, into feeling deeply connected and in harmony with the planet, all the people on it, and the Universe we lived in. Even when I had bad days I still felt connected, and I never really felt alone anymore.

In my new sober life, I noticed that I felt different about a lot of things. Like, my old classmates for instance. Now, when I heard that someone had just landed a huge promotion, bought a gorgeous new home, or won a prestigious award, I didn't feel small and stupid in comparison. I didn't feel the "comparison" at all, so I also didn't feel jealous or like I was doing something wrong. I was happy for them because I didn't feel like their achievements had somehow overshadowed my own.

I had shifted my mindset, in a fundamental way. I was no longer achievement oriented. I was now relationship oriented.

I've studied this shift in depth in all the years since and I've only become more convinced that, as a culture, we are all moving from an achievement oriented mindset to one that is relationship oriented. In my opinion, this is a huge improvement. Not only does it emotionally feel a lot better, but it's also more efficient.

Consider this: When someone is achievement oriented, by necessity, they feel alone and cut off from others. "Achievement" means "win" to most people, and in order to win, you have to beat someone else. For winners to exist, there must be losers. So, again by necessity, everything achievement oriented people do comes down to trying to do it better than someone else, or trying to grab resources that are scarce so that they can get more than their neighbor. This mentality breeds a constant energy of unhealthy competition, aggression, ruthlessness, and inadequacy. For whenever you "win" something, it quickly becomes not enough and then you need to win something else just to stay on top.

If you're wondering what an achievement oriented culture looks like after it's been allowed to run rampant for years on end, look no further than Hollywood or the political scene in Washington, D.C. People who engage in gossip and slander, point fingers, denounce, boast, and threaten and intimidate others are all very much a part of any achievement oriented scene. In this kind of culture, aging and illness are unacceptable, emotions are suppressed, and compassion is seen as a weakness.

This is also the overall dominant culture of the current Western world.

And this is why so many writers and artists (especially us Highly Sensitive folk) are so turned off by marketing. Almost all the marketing messages you see coming out of an achievement oriented culture focus on youth and beauty, or wealth and status.

However, things *are* changing.

As more people across the planet "wake up" as a result of the multiple crisis points we're hitting with foreign relations, technology, the environment, and identity issues, the more we see this shift occurring all around the globe. The achievement oriented system isn't working anymore. In fact, it's irrevocably broken. We're being pushed to change our ways and change them fast. We are—because we really have no other choice—now moving into a relationship oriented world.

In a relationship oriented culture, everyone understands that "we are all connected" isn't just a feel-good saying to throw around, it's real, serious business. "We are all connected" means that if you dump toxic waste in the ocean, it affects *everyone*. It means that if kids are getting bullied, that negative energy is being spread through all the young people in our society, and poisoning every one of us.

Relationship oriented marketing looks a lot different from achievement oriented marketing. When you're focused on relationships, the highest priority is working toward what is helpful for all parties involved at this time. So, authors aren't trying to push their book down everyone's throat in the desperate attempt to rack up high sales figures. Instead, they're carefully crafting their message to reach the people who will actually be helped by reading their book. Coaches, editors, and publishers aren't trying to do a "hard sell" on potential clients to rake in as much income as they can. Instead, they're devoting their energy to being thoughtful about entering into new client relationships, knowing that the highest priority is building a relationship that helps both parties grow and evolve.

Relationship oriented marketing extends to all levels of the marketing experience: Book launches, getting reviews, social media, and advertising. When a writer has a relationship oriented mindset, they're focused on authenticity, personal values, and contributing their artistic gifts to be of service to others. The fear state that is triggered by feeling inadequate in some way, or by some part of the marketing process not unfolding according to expectations, is largely dissolved, and the author can reclaim that energy and put it to good use: toward feeling empowered and of service to the community.

Once I shifted from an achievement oriented mindset to a relationship oriented mindset I was able to look back on my experiences in Seattle (working in the bookstore by day and carousing through the dive bars by night) as the exact right place I needed to be at that time. Those experiences were part of my journey, and part of the learning process I needed to go through in order to be of service to the world. It didn't matter that I wasn't in medical school or law school, or getting my PhD. I was never supposed to be doing those things. My unique gifts flowered in a different way. And I needed just those unique gifts to play the part I was destined to play in all my future relationships.

Moving into a relationship oriented mindset around your marketing practice is going to be an ongoing process. Many people won't understand what you're doing or why you're doing it. For those who are still on the achievement oriented system of doing things, your new relationship oriented mindset is most probably going to seem threatening. They might feel you're opening yourself up to being "walked on" or putting yourself at a disadvantage in some way because you're embracing a mode of trusting people and having faith in a larger plan. That's okay. Your mission is not to convert everyone around you to the relationship oriented mindset. Your mission is to concentrate on your own marketing practice and not worry about what others are doing.

When you have a few minutes to sit and think deeply, jot down your answers to these questions to see how you could move more effectively into a relationship oriented marketing practice:

Do you normally read and review books for other authors? If so, do you expect to receive something back immediately in return?

How good are you at "receiving"? For instance, if someone offers to carry a bag for you or help with the dishes, is your automatic response to refuse the offer of service they're making? If so, why might that be? Do you feel like you might be in someone else's debt if you accept help?

When you think about selling your book do you envision high sales numbers and winning prestigious awards? Or do you envision the actual people who might read your book? Have you imagined what kind of emotions and thoughts those people might experience while reading your book? Have you imagined what kind of inner changes they might go through as a result of reading your book?

Do you see your writing career as a higher calling or a life purpose? Do you see it as a right and perfect piece of your life's journey? Or do you see it as something you are just "trying to do" to see if it will "work"?

If you released your book and no one bought it, would you still keep writing? What if only five people bought it, but each person reached out and let you know that it really changed their life? How would you feel then?

Part Two
Believing the Magic

Chapter 9
The Three Magic Keys: Intrigue, Resonance, and Teaching

I t was a warm Sunday afternoon in late September and I was spending the last of my weekend doing my favorite thing in the world: shopping for books. Every year the San Francisco Library held its big annual book sale in the fall and I never missed it. I always made sure to attend on the last day of the sale too, when every book was marked down to one dollar.

The sale is held at Fort Mason, in a huge building that feels a lot like a warehouse, near San Francisco's famous Fisherman's Wharf. When I arrived, I stood at the entrance for a few moments to savor what lay before me. I saw table after table of books spread out as far as the eye could see. Every imaginable category had been included. People slowly and quietly pushed around shopping carts that were already full, adding even more to the stacks they had selected. I knew a lot of these people were probably resellers, here for the once-a-year opportunity to get bargain finds that the library needed to liquidate in order to make room for incoming titles.

I didn't have a shopping cart, only one $20 bill with me. One of my library sale rules was that I only brought a single twenty, and no other form of payment, to ensure that I stayed within reasonable book-buying bounds. At one dollar a book, I could afford to go wild. But as a committed bibliophile, my shelves at home were already groaning under the weight of my ever-expanding to-be-read pile. If I brought home 20 books (and I definitely would, I had never NOT spent every dollar of that twenty) it would be more than enough.

As I picked my way through the tables, reading the blurb on the back of this book or that one, I let myself enter that dreamy-yet-concentrated space I always go into when I'm browsing for books. This is the exact opposite mindset I have when searching for a specific title. In that case, I jump on Amazon, find it, and push the buy button, all in under two minutes. The energy of browsing a library sale is much different. To me, it's more like surfing through the Kindle store, with no set expectations, but only a loose budget to be spent on whatever catches my fancy.

So…what would catch my fancy? And how is the fancy of most readers caught? As a consumer, I was passingly curious about this phenomenon, but as a writer, and now a self-published author, I was seriously interested.

Let's go back to the library sale to see if I found any answers there.

First, I checked out the self-help and spirituality section, one of my favorites. I immediately spotted a copy of Marianne Williamson's *Return to Love*, an older book but a classic, and one that I had been meaning to read for years. I love Marianne and have listened to many of her talks online. I think of her as a wise teacher and someone I very much admire. I knew *A Return to Love* would have a lot to teach me. I scooped up Marianne's book and kept moving.

Next, I meandered over to the history section, another topic I enjoy. After picking through the titles on Russian history, I found a book on Rasputin and smiled to myself. I had been curious about Rasputin for a long time. I loved Russian history and he seemed to always make an appearance somewhere. I had heard tons of rumors about the man—that he was a mystic, a psychic, a prophet, a con artist, and nearly impossible to kill. He had shadowy origins and more layers than an onion. Every time his name came up I was intrigued. I wanted more. I added the book to my growing pile.

After that I ended up in memoir, another category close to my heart. I saw Joan Didion's *Year of Magical Thinking* and slowly picked it up, paging through it thoughtfully. I had heard of this book too. I knew it was the book Didion wrote about her experiences in the year after losing her husband to a sudden heart attack. As I read the blurb I found myself nodding. It was a book about loss, and grief, and all the thousands of different facets of each. I had just lost my dad to brain cancer a few months ago. I could definitely relate. This was a story that would resonate with me, deeply. I decided to buy that one too.

Out of the bazillion books available at this sale, I immediately picked these three. Why? Because each book offered me something specific. Each book held a magic key that pushed me to take a chance on it. Three books, three magic keys. I believe these three magic keys translate into the three big reasons most readers take a chance on buying the books they do. To see them in action, let's look at each book I chose again:

- **The Book on Rasputin** – I bought this book because I was *intrigued* by the subject. I had heard interesting things that piqued my curiosity. How did these pieces fit together? I wanted to know the answer to the puzzle. I felt that reading the book would be an enjoyable experience because it would satisfy this feeling of intrigue I had about the topic it discussed.
- **Joan Didion's *Year of Magical Thinking*** – This is a book that immediately *resonated* with me. The author had gone through a life event that was very similar to a life event I had just experienced, and it was a big intense life event that felt like it had cast me adrift, and

made me feel small and alone. Didion's book offered me hope and promise: I wasn't alone, and it would get better.

- **Marianne Williamson's *A Return to Love*** – I love to learn, and spirituality is one of my favorite topics to learn about. Marianne has a great reputation as a teacher and I had no doubt that her book would *teach me something* new and useful. In fact, I'm always on the lookout for books that can *teach me something*. The teacher doesn't have to be famous or have guru-like status, they just have to let me know pretty quickly what their teachings are about and how they could improve my life in some way.

And those are the three magic keys that push readers to take a chance on a book:

- *Intrigue*
- *Resonance*
- *Education*

If you're serious about learning how to market your book well, it will be helpful for you to take some time to think about which of these three magic keys work for your book. It's also good to remember that just because your book might mainly appeal in one area, that doesn't mean that the other two don't apply. Let's look in depth at each one:

Intrigue

Horror novels are a good example of a genre that falls under "intrigue." Think of any Stephen King novel: the hook is always that this mysterious, somewhat sinister thing is going on and there's even more mysterious, sinister stuff behind it. The same goes for Shirley Jackson's horror novels like *We Have Always Lived in the Castle* or *The Haunting of Hill House*. The premise is always that something weird is going on, and whatever it is, it's intriguing.

Intrigue can apply to more than horror though. Take the case of the nonfiction book *Proof of Heaven* by Dr. Eben Alexander: a highly trained neurosurgeon goes into a severe coma for seven days and is basically brain dead, and then comes back to tell the story of his near-death experience. The intrigue hook in this example is actually not the near-death experience, it's the fact that it was experienced by a highly trained neurosurgeon, someone who is extremely rational and knows the scientific side of the brain and STILL says that he saw heaven. How do *those* pieces fit together? That's intrigue at work.

Resonance

Like intrigue, resonance can apply to fiction or nonfiction. A middle grade fantasy novel about a young girl who is bullied at school has massive resonance potential. A memoir about drug addiction, childhood abuse, or depression has resonance potential too. Any story that deals with difficult emotional issues taps into the potential for deep resonance the story will have with other people who have gone through those types of experiences.

Interestingly, the biggest disadvantage I usually see with this type of work is that the authors sometimes still carry shame about their experience and assume that "no one will want to read it," "no one will get it," or "everyone" will find out that the writer is flawed, damaged, or irreversibly broken. Ironically enough, that shame and those fears are exactly what readers connect with the most. Joan Didion detailed how her husband's death pushed her past a mental breaking point into clinical insanity. Did I judge her? Nope. I was right there with her. Once you've experienced extreme grief, you know how crazy it can get. I was just glad someone else had the guts to be real and talk about it.

Education

Obviously almost all self-help and "how-to" books fall into this category, but education can also encompass fiction, memoir, and any other kind of book. One of my clients was a young woman writing a semi-fictionalized account of her grandfather's experience growing up in China before World War II and how the rest of his life unfolded after that. During one of our meetings she expressed to me that she was feeling disheartened because she assumed that the only people interested in reading her book would be members of the Chinese-American community. I let her know that wasn't the case at all. Even though her story was going to come out as "fiction" I knew there were tons of people out there like me, readers who explored authors who talked about what it was like to grow up in a different country, a different culture, or a different time. These diverse experiences had something to teach me. I had no doubt about that.

Your book might not be a manual on how to learn to play guitar in 90 days, but that doesn't mean that it doesn't have a strong educational aspect to it. Think about who could learn from the message behind your book and you're well on your way to finding the teaching in your work.

∼

You can use these simple exercises to determine which of the three magic keys—intrigue, resonance, and education—works for your book:

Are there any mysterious elements to your story? Does the supernatural or the sinister make an appearance? Are there pieces to your story that don't seem to fit together on the surface, but once you read the story everything makes perfect sense? If you answered a strong "yes" to any of these questions, you might have a story that holds the magic key of intrigue.

Are you writing a memoir about a difficult or exciting period in your life? Or maybe just your life as a whole and everything crazy you've gone through? Are you writing about an issue that has made you feel isolated or alone in the past? Or that you've been ashamed to share with anyone else? Do any of your characters feel a strong sense of shame because of things that happen to them in your story? Do they feel isolated or alone? If you answered yes to more than one of these questions, resonance *might be the magic key to your story.*

Would you say that someone's worldview might be broadened after reading your story? Would you say that your story might help someone to move out of judgment around a certain topic and into acceptance or even forgiveness? Do you think your story might have the power to shine a little light into dark and ignorant places? Does your story deal with things you've learned that you wish you knew when you were younger or less experienced? If so, your story probably has a lot to teach people and falls under education.

Chapter 10
A New Definition of Family: How to Network like a Heart-Centered Human Being

For the first few years I was on Twitter no one believed me when I told them that was where I got all my clients. Or they said, "But everyone hates spam!"

Well, I wasn't spamming people and I was very definitely getting clients. In fact, that was how I built my online coaching business in the beginning, solely from people finding my blog through Twitter.

These days, when it's apparent that I do actually have a legitimate business and a big presence on Twitter, people ask me how I do it. Because as we all know, one thing hasn't changed. People still hate spam.

But I never have spammed people and I never will. I hate spam too. In fact, I do very little to promote my services at all on Twitter. Instead, I look for writers and artists who I feel might be part of my family. And then I reach out to them, start a conversation, and see if I can be of help in some way.

What do I mean when I say "family"? I mean it the way Mafia guys use the word.

A year or two ago I read a great memoir by an old school Mafia boss, Joseph Bonnano. I've never been much interested in pursuing a life of crime, but Joe Bonnano's story resonated with me on a few different levels. He talked about the origins of the "family" as it came to be known in American mob culture, and how it stemmed from Sicilian communities back in the Old World. Back in Old World Sicily, life was extremely hard. Between poverty, oppressive governments, and constant violence and war, people had to make do with very little and they had to make that little stretch a long way. So, early on, Sicilians figured out they stood a much better chance of making it if they banded together in communities, an extended kind of "family," and all looked out for each other, and tried to help each other, whenever they could.

Sicilian immigrants brought this structure of interlocking clans, and the mindset that went with it, when they ventured into the New World, where life was just as hard. It was tough to make it in a new place where you didn't speak the language, you were still dirt poor, and most of the established population was either suspicious or resentful of you. The "family" structure was needed more than ever.

My theory is that it's the same for writers.

It's tough to be a writer in today's world. Yes, opportunities are open to us like never before, but we still have to contend with swimming in an ocean of media and information, made up of millions of people who are trying to get their voices heard. Not to mention that being an indie writer today really means that you're a solopreneur. Sometimes you have to wear ALL the hats: writer, formatter, designer, marketer, salesperson, IT person, speaker, teacher, and most importantly, lifelong learner.

Joe Bonnano rose through the ranks to become the head of one of the most powerful Mafia families in New York, and he didn't do it trying to do everything on his own. Joe's secret was that he looked out for other people. He took care of the members of his family. He stayed conscious about giving anyone who needed it an opportunity they might not otherwise have gotten.

Again, it's the same for writers.

We need to look out for each other.

This is the new kind of networking that is the *only* way any of us stand a chance in the current online world. In decades past, the focus might have been on competition, domination, winning at all costs and doing whatever it takes to get there, but that model is outdated, and frankly, just doesn't work anymore. There is simply too much information available. There are too many options on offer at any given moment for people to waste their time with a lone wolf who's only out for himself.

We have to start thinking of our "family" first. For Highly Sensitive Writers, your family is anyone who is on your creative wavelength.

That doesn't mean that if you write cozy mysteries you can only hang out with the other cozy mystery people. It means that if you hold values like openness, integrity, fun, curiosity, and positivity, then you search out other writer folks who hold those same values. And, if you're doing most of your socializing online, it's actually pretty easy. Writers usually list exactly what they're all about in their Twitter bio, or on the About page of their blog, or somewhere on the any number of social media profiles they've posted online.

I can't tell you how many clients I've gained simply because I started following someone on Twitter, read one of their Tweets, and then responded to them in a genuine way. Maybe they were having a bad day, or maybe they just wanted to share the first line of their work-in-progress. If something catches my eye and it resonates with me, I usually reach out. Sometimes these conversations lead to nothing, but sometimes they go deeper and my new writer friend and I find out we have a lot in common. Then we move the conversation to email. Sometimes they become a client, and sometimes they turn into a wonderful friend, but no matter what the end result is, the take-away is the same. I didn't start talking to that person on Twitter because I was fishing for business. I started talking to them because I recognized that they might be part of my writer "family" and I wanted to see if I could help them in some way.

Many people are hesitant to offer help to strangers because they're worried about being taken advantage of, or of giving more than they get back. I'll be upfront about the family mindset: a lot of times you will give without getting anything back. But, to take another lesson from Joe Bonnano, just because you don't personally benefit from an interaction or exchange, doesn't mean it wasn't worth it. Because the community always benefits. Every single time you give something of yourself, every time you go out of your way to help someone in your "family" get an opportunity they otherwise wouldn't have had access to, the community benefits, always. You are a part of that community, and if your community is healthy and thriving and growing, *you* will benefit, whether you are conscious of it or not.

So, how can you start giving to your community? How can you begin to support your writing "family" in a very real way?

You can start by reading.

The number one thing any writer needs, hopes for, prays for, and bends over backwards for, are new readers. If you find a writer who looks like they might be part of your family—whether that be through social media, or through a blog or email newsletter, or even if you just see a sign at your neighborhood bookstore for a local author event that weekend—pick up their book and *read it*. Then leave them a review. Then talk about how much you liked their book on social media. Then send them a message or email to tell them you liked their book and that they're doing a great job. If you're reading this book then you're a writer yourself and you know how badly we need to hear encouragement. You know how a few kind words can make all the difference between deciding to carry on or giving it up for good.

Sometimes this won't lead to much besides you discovering a book you like and doing a good turn for another writer. But sometimes it will lead to a great friendship, or another writer in your corner on social media who makes sure to share your posts, and who tweets about your book when it comes out, and who shows up in your inbox on some dark morning to tell you to keep going when you really need to hear it.

This is how you begin to find and nurture your writing family. It doesn't happen overnight. And yes, you will make mistakes. You will think you have a lot in common with some writers and then nothing will come of the relationship. That's normal. Joseph Bonnano didn't end up with a towering pyramid of people who all had his back in just a couple of weeks. He spent years cultivating relationships, doing favors for people, putting in a good word here and there, and in general working his ass off to serve the community of his "family."

This brings me to the last objection I always hear from writers about networking. "But it feels so fake," they say. "I don't want to be a part of anything fake like that." And the only answer I can give, is that it will be fake, if you make it fake. If you're reaching out to people you honestly couldn't care less about, then it will be fake. If you're only talking to someone online or in the real world because you think they might be able to serve you in the future, then again, that's a choice you're making and a particular energy that you're bringing to the table. It doesn't have to be like that. But the choice is up to you.

Reaching out to strangers is going to make you feel vulnerable, there is no way around that. But finding your place in your writing family and helping to grow that community will make you feel stronger than you ever imagined.

~

Here are some ways you can get started on finding your writing family:

Start a social media account on a platform that you've never tried before. Give it an honest chance and look around to see how it works. Find three authors who you think you might like. Reach out to all of them and tell them that their work looks interesting to you. Pick one of them and buy their book. Actually read it.

If you haven't already, make an account on Goodreads and look around at all the different reading groups. Join one. If you're already on Goodreads, join a new group. Post a message in the group asking for recommendations on a particular topic.

Pick a book you've read in the last year that you really liked. Find the author on social media and give them a shout out. It doesn't matter if they're really famous. Both Margaret Atwood and Amy Tan have responded to me on social media when I sent them a compliment. You never know what might happen.

Chapter 11
Social Media: Setting Boundaries and Protecting Your Energy

I n 2013 I was not on Facebook. I hadn't started my blog yet and I wasn't on Twitter either. In fact, I wasn't on any sort of social media. A lot of people questioned me about this, pretty much all the time. I had friends who were on Facebook all day long and even when I met new people they asked if I was on social media. A curious thing started to happen, the more people asked me why I wasn't on social media, the more resistant I felt myself becoming toward it.

This was not a huge mystery to me. I have been a private person all my life. I have this really weird introvert vs. mentor thing going on with my energy. One side of me is extremely private. Whenever I feel threatened in any way, I immediately withdraw. I tend not to share my emotions with people until I've had at least a few weeks to process them. I live most of my life in an inner world that no one else ever sees. That's the introvert side.

Then there's the mentor side, and that side also has a bit of the performer thrown in (more introverts are performer-types than you would guess). The mentor in me loves sharing my personal stories in the hope that they'll make other people feel not so alone and serve as a connecting bridge between people. The performer in me will provide all the gory, gritty details to make it a really good story, too.

So, I want to share my stories with the whole world. At the same time, I don't want anyone to look at me.

This is why so much resistance showed up whenever I thought about getting on social media.

Well, I decided to give it a go. I signed up for a Facebook account and made a page. *That wasn't so bad*, I thought. Next, I found some of my friends and sent them friend requests. *That wasn't so bad either*, I chuckled to myself. Maybe I was making too big a deal out of all of this.

Then a couple of weeks passed and my Facebook train really got rolling and I found myself HORRIFIED at what I had jumped into.

People I hadn't seen since high school started sending me friend requests, and while it was nice to connect with some of these people, some of the others I was ambivalent about, to say the least. Then Facebook started making suggestions about other people I might want to "friend." A lot of these friend-of-a-friend connections were people that I *did* know from past friend groups, but something weird or awkward or just plain bad had gone down between the two of us and I had hoped I would never have to see them again. Suddenly, Facebook was floating these people in front of me every time I logged in, nudging me to be friends with them.

Then, I noticed something else. Perfectly lovely people who I had just had brunch with on Saturday and who had told me delightful stories about their playful cat were showing up in my stream ranting about everything under the sun, in long irate blocks of text that sounded like a crazy person had written them. Other people were exposing graphic details about their lives that I really didn't want to know. Still others were "poking" me and asking me to play Candy Crush with them.

I was seriously overwhelmed. I had that same feeling I always get when I go to a five-hour-long party where everyone is drunk except for me. Drained, dumped on, and defeated.

My first reaction was to blame social media, shut down my Facebook account, and never come back. Instead, I took a few days to chill out and think about the situation and I realized a few very important things.

Social Media Is a Big Party

There is a very good reason most introverts and Highly Sensitive People feel overwhelmed by social media when they first start using it, because it is exactly like walking into a big party. Not only that, it's actually like walking into the middle of New Orleans during Mardi Gras. It feels like EVERYONE is there. It is also obvious that the "virtual" nature of the experience gives people the same lowered inhibitions that too much alcohol brings on. People feel like they're operating in a space that isn't real and doesn't deliver the same consequences as the rest of life (and in that, they would be mostly right). So, they yell at each other and say awful things they would never say to someone's face if they were sitting across from them in real life. They also over-share, big time.

This is why it's so essential to remember that it takes some time to get used to social media, and *to find the spaces in which you most enjoy playing*. As a Highly Sensitive Writer, you are not going to have fun milling out in the streets in the middle of the big parade with all the crazy drunk people. You might have fun though, if you find your own little nook that's off the beaten path and populated with kindred souls. Your safe space might be a private Facebook group for writers or an online forum for Highly Sensitive People. Wherever it is that you feel good in the online world, the important thing is that you don't hesitate to go there, and ignore all the rest of the noise.

And, the other thing to remember in order to keep your sanity intact with social media is…

We Are the Ones in Charge of Our Boundaries

This is a tough one. So many Highly Sensitive Writers grow up as the caretaker in our families. Many of us seamlessly dovetail into codependent relationships as adults too, in order to keep playing out that caretaker role. We are extremely skilled at picking up on other people's emotions, down to every subtle nuance on the emotional scale. It's an easy jump to go from *picking up on* someone else's emotions to *trying to manage* someone else's emotions, and this is where we get into trouble.

When we see that Facebook post from the person who is spilling their guts about a big messy breakup they just went through, or another workplace drama, or just ranting and raving about the world in general, we feel a strong compulsion to jump in there and help. And even if we have pretty good boundaries and we're somewhat adept at not taking on responsibility for someone else's experience, we're still highly empathic. We read the post and we immediately absorb the rage, the blame, the repressed sorrow, the concentrated dose of fear. Then we feel like crap. That's why— even though we've done a good job of finding our safe space off the main Mardi Gras strip—navigating through the crowd to get there can still leave us feeling exhausted and ill.

However, it is possible to put a few simple rules in place to make sure your boundaries stay strong.

On Facebook

Rule number one: Only accept Friend requests from people you like and feel comfortable with.

Unfriend anyone who violates rule number one.

Unfollow anyone who you still like, but whose updates you aren't interested in for whatever reason.

I'm friends with hundreds of people on Facebook and I've unfollowed many of them. If someone *routinely* posts things that feel "low-energy" to me (blaming, whining, complaining, boasting, or any other variation of ego-centric) I unfollow them.

On Twitter

Don't ever read your stream. Instead, make LISTS and use them!

Make a "writer friends" list, an "inspiring people" list, a "book-store" list, a "help with marketing list," and any other list you can think of and *only read tweets from your lists*. This is the number one rule I teach writers who are getting started on Twitter. If you thought your Facebook stream was a river of nonstop information, Twitter is like Niagara Falls. It's just too much for any one person to keep up with and it's too unfiltered. Learning how to use lists will change your entire Twitter experience.

When I log in to Twitter I check my writer friends list first thing to see what's going on with my community that day. These are mostly people I have met through the blogosphere or in real life. They are lovely, intelligent, compassionate people who share interesting and useful information about writing. I then check my "bookstores" and "libraries" list for something fun to retweet. Then I'm done. I've successfully jumped into Twitter for 20 minutes and gotten back out again unscathed by trolls, reactionary anger and ranting, or weird spammy sexbots.

You have to lay out the parameters of your own boundaries. The key is to take conscious responsibility for your own boundaries on social media *all the time*. YOU choose who you engage with and how. YOU choose what you view and what you allow into your precious mental space. YOU choose what you share with other people and what kind of impact on their day you want to have.

This brings us to one last issue Highly Sensitive Writers need to be aware of...

Feeling Exposed

The feeling of being exposed is another frequent complaint I get from my clients about why they don't want to participate in the social media world. I'm an introvert and an HSP too, so I get it. I feel highly uncomfortable sharing details about my personal life with people who are not in my inner circle, and my inner circle is very, very small.

This is why it's so important to remember that you don't have to share anything you don't want to. For example, my husband and I have a strict policy when it comes to our son. We do not post pictures of him on social media, ever. We believe that's a choice our son should make for himself, and he's not yet old enough to make that choice. So, in the meantime, we just don't do it. Now, I'm not saying everyone should adopt this choice or strategy. What I am saying is that every person has to decide for themselves what they are comfortable with and continuously check in to re-evaluate that choice.

My husband also doesn't want pictures of himself on social media and I respect that. So, the end result is that I'm a writer and a writing coach with two Facebook pages (personal and author page), a Twitter account, a Pinterest account, a LinkedIn account, a Youtube channel, a website and a blog, and nowhere online will you find pictures of my husband or son. You will also not find many personal pictures of me besides the official headshots I've used throughout the years across my platform. Missing too are daily updates on what I'm having for dinner, where I'm going on vacation, or the new pair of shoes I just bought. I don't feel comfortable sharing that kind of stuff online so I don't.

Regardless, I still have over 50k followers on Twitter and I spend at least 20-30 minutes a day on social media five days a week. If I don't discuss my family or my day-to-day life, then what do I talk about?

Writing.

Oh…and also, books.

You get to choose what you talk about and what you share with people. But as a Highly Sensitive Writer, the most important choice is always: *who is going to get your energy today?* Being conscious of that choice can transform a draining social media experience into one that's actually inspiring.

These social media exercises can be done over the course of a week or two. Start slowly and go slowly. If you're feeling overwhelmed, take a break for a day or two and come back to it.

Pick a social media platform that you've never used (something you feel resistant to would be best) and jump online right now and make an account.

Poke around inside your newly-made account and explore. Be brave and put yourself out there a little bit in some way.

If you already have a Twitter account, spend 20-30 minutes browsing around. Look at awesome writing accounts like NaNoWriMo, Jane Friedman, K.M. Weiland, and Writer Unboxed. Look at their follower lists and see if anyone looks like they're on your wavelength. Try following 50 new people or even 100 new people to see what happens.

As long as you're on Twitter, keep browsing and reading bios. Whenever you stumble across someone's bio that speaks to you in some way tweet them and tell them it resonated with you. Maybe they love William Faulkner too, or you recognize the quote they're using. Whatever it is, reach out and TELL them you liked their thing or connected with their thing or think their thing is cool. Again, see what happens.

Now, jump on Facebook (or make an account if you don't have one already) and get busy. Clean up your stream by unfollowing anyone negative. Browse around the groups by searching for terms like "introvert" and "writer" and join a group or two to see what they have to offer. Read the group posts and make comments on things that resonate with you or compliment people who shared something great. And then, you already know what I'm going to say...see what happens!

Chapter 12

Standing Tall: Strengthening Your Author Website with Your Own Personal Power

O ne day I was tripping through Twitter land, scrolling through all of the possible new friends I could make, when I experienced that beautiful moment of finding someone I just knew was a kindred soul. She wrote dark, weird fiction, loved cats, and said she had been a tree spirit in another life. I was so intrigued. I happened to be obsessed with dark, weird fiction at the time and I couldn't wait to find out more about her and her writing.

Hmmm…I couldn't see much from her profile pic though. She was turned half away from the camera and it was kind of grainy. *Okay, I'll just click through to her website*, I thought. But when I landed there I was even more disappointed.

She had a blog going but she hadn't updated it in ages. There was no sign-up box to follow her blog updates and no more detailed information about her writing at all. Her About Page repeated the same exact text that I'd seen on her Twitter bio and that was it. I couldn't even get her full name. Her Twitter handle listed her as something like @twinklestar14839 and her blog domain name was writing4ever2u.com.

This sounds like a plot twist in a James Patterson thriller.

Mysterious character makes an intriguing entrance only to vanish into virtual thin air.

Sadly, I know this writer probably wasn't trying to be deliberately evasive.

Her online presence just needed a lot of work.

For people who have chosen the rational, ordered, very-much-culturally-approved path of traditional business, building a strong online presence is something taken for granted. Mainstream business people usually have no problem providing the world with a nice big headshot and contact options prominently displayed, while also learning how to network like a pro on LinkedIn.

For Highly Sensitive Writers, this process can be much more difficult.

We Highly Sensitive Writers have usually spent much of our lives hiding. We were the weird kid in school. We were the nerdy kid who was bullied. We were the quiet, shy, awkward, eccentric, bookish, sensitive, emotional kid who found out early on that it was better to stay invisible and fly under the radar. The more we sunk into the shadows, the more other people left us alone and the less we got hurt.

So, as adults, when we're trying to do this whole writing thing —maybe even have a whole writing *career*—it can be hard to overcome those old habits and defense mechanisms. It can feel extremely uncomfortable to put our full name online, to announce that we're a writer, to put up a picture of ourselves that is big and clear and noticeable, and to give strangers the option of getting in touch.

(As a quick aside: There can be a lot of controversy in the writing community about whether to write under a pen name or not. In my opinion, it is perfectly fine to write under a pen name. I do not consider this a form of hiding. However, if you choose to write under a pen name, then it is essential that you treat that name and that identity just like you would if it was your own. It's important to be just as out and proud with that name on your writer's website.)

Now, to return to the theme of hiding. Most Highly Sensitive Writers "hide" online in three different ways. They might employ one strategy at a time, or use two, or even all three, in combination.

Profile Picture

A writer who is uneasy about putting herself out there usually has a profile picture that is too small, too grainy, or too dim. Some writers use pictures that show them with hair covering half their face, wearing big sunglasses, or with someone else in the picture (so it's unclear who they are and who the friend is). Sometimes the writer's profile pic isn't even a pic of them at all, it's a picture of a cat or a turtle or something. This is okay for your personal Facebook page picture, but for your Facebook author page, Twitter, LinkedIn, and your writer's website, a profile pic that is a good headshot of you is the best.

A good profile pic should be a clear, somewhat close-up picture of your face or the upper portion of your body. It should be full on or only slightly angled to the side. It should also be a picture of you as you actually look now, not ten years ago or wearing a bunch of makeup and sexy clothes that you don't normally wear. If you DO normally wear a bunch of makeup and sexy clothes then that's the way to go. What's important is that your profile pic looks like you *as you are right now*, the real authentic you.

The test of a great profile pic is that if someone saw your picture online and then passed you on the street a few minutes later they would be able to recognize you.

The difference between a good and bad profile pic is the difference between striding into a room with confidence, and slinking into a room hoping not to be noticed. It's not about getting the "perfect picture." It's about working with issues of self-worth. It's okay if you don't feel one hundred percent confident about your profile picture. It's okay if you feel self-conscious about your skin, or your teeth, or your gray hair. The goal is not to transform yourself into a photoshopped miracle of physical perfection. The goal is to accept yourself as you are and walk forward into the online world as that person.

I never like any new profile picture I take. I always feel like I look nerdy. I always have the urge to ditch the glasses and glam myself up for the camera. But in real life I wear glasses every day and I never wear makeup. In real life, I'm just not all that glamorous. I usually don't feel self-conscious about that until it comes time to take a new profile picture. Then I feel like I should be everything I'm not.

So far, every time I've worked through it. I've taken a picture that authentically looks like me. Every time, I eventually grow to like it.

Sign-Up Box

This one sounds so easy you might question why I'm even mentioning it, but you wouldn't believe the number of writers' websites and blogs I visit that don't have one prominently displayed. Yes, I know that a lot of WordPress sites will offer up the little box if you hover the mouse in the right corner, but not a lot of other people know that or remember it if they're in a hurry. A writer should *always* have a 'Subscribe Here' button featured big and obvious in the sidebar, so that it's one of the first things a new reader sees.

In our current online world, it's hard to keep track of people. Even if someone is following you on Twitter, Facebook, or Instagram, it's very likely your posts will get lost in their stream. And there is no way you can expect someone to just "remember" your blog and keep checking back in for updates. It might be old-fashioned, but getting notifications by email goes a long way toward making sure you stay connected, and they stay up-to-date on your news.

Sometimes it's a simple matter of writers not realizing their sign-up boxes aren't as big and clear as they should be, but a lot of the time there is an unconscious fear coming up around the issue, too. When people start signing up to receive your updates, it's typical to then start feeling pressure about having to deliver. Many writers conveniently "forget" to put a sign-up box on their website because, unconsciously, they don't want to feel like there are readers out there depending on them to write something good. But you don't have to continue to prove yourself to your readers. Either they will like what you're putting out, or they won't. It's not personal and it doesn't have to be. The ones who are meant to stick with you will stick.

Contact Page

One of my clients told me that he desperately wanted to find his creative tribe. I suggested that every morning he say out loud: "If there is someone I'm supposed to meet today, send them to me. I am ready." He liked the idea but had some misgivings. He had tried setting intentions like that before, he said, and every time he did he experienced excitement, but also panic. What if the people who showed up brought a whole bunch of baggage with them? What if they were going to expect things of him? Or judge him? What if they turned out to be like a few people he'd had bad experiences with in the past, narcissists, abusers, and the like?

The fear and panic that my client was experiencing is a common unconscious reason that a lot of Highly Sensitive Writers also conveniently "forget" to set up a functioning, easy-to-find contact option on their website. Because most of us are intuitives and empaths, we've been fending difficult people off our whole lives. Most of us have experienced our fair share of toxic people and it doesn't seem that we have to go looking for them either. They find us. No matter where we are or how we try to hide.

For many of us, this is also one of the big obstacles we deal with when we think about putting any sort of personal nonfiction or memoir out into the world. We want to help people through our work...but oh, we are so over those energy vampires who keep showing up at our door. Won't a contact page (or our book) be just one more beacon to draw them our way?

Well, yes, it can be. But this is where boundary work comes in again.

People will contact you. That's the whole point of a contact page. You want to make it easy for people to get in touch with you so that they can offer you kind words, a hand extended in friendship, or even artistic opportunities for collaboration. It's up to you to put boundaries in place before you put up that contact page though. So, if someone contacts you and pours out their life story in the very first email and you start getting that shrinking, panicky feeling that they're invading your energetic space, it's not that big of a deal. Because you're able to either a) delete their email or b) send them a short and closed response that invites no further contact and c) not feel very guilty about doing either.

It's *your* website. You have the power. You can delete hostile blog comments and weird emails from strangers. You don't have to engage with anyone that you don't want to talk to. You don't need a reason. You can trust your gut that you're getting a "no" on this person.

Once your boundaries are firmly in place, you can give yourself permission to let a strong website work for you. A strong website lets new readers know who you are, what you look like, and what you're all about within a few seconds of them landing on your homepage. It also shows them clearly where to go to get their hands on your work and learn more about you as a writer and a person. A strong website is the virtual equivalent of you feeling comfortable in your body, standing up straight, speaking clearly, and making steady eye contact as you talk to people at the party.

No, it won't be easy right away. But personal growth work never is. That's why it's fun.

～

Try these exercises to get started building (or strengthening) your online presence:

Do you have a website already? If you don't, make plans to set one up. Decide on a domain name and brainstorm on how you can find a website support person to help you. Quick tip: Googling "WordPress author assistant" will bring up lots of good results.

Evaluate the profile picture you're using on your social media accounts. Is it a picture of 1) your full face 2) in good light that 3) looks like the real you? If not, make plans to change that. You don't need to hire a professional to get a good picture. Ask a friend to join you in the park for a photo shoot using their iPhone and offer to buy them lunch afterward for their time and help.

If you already have a website, pretend you are a totally new reader who has just landed on it for the first time. Is it easy to find your author name? Is it easy to see what you look like? Is it easy to sign up for updates? Is it easy to learn more about you and your writing? Is it easy to buy your books? Keep a notepad handy while you're doing this exercise and jot down a list of items that could be improved. Use the quick tip from our first exercise and Google "WordPress author assistant" (or just "virtual author assistant") to see if you can find someone to help you make the changes you want to see.

Chapter 13
The Art of the Freebie: Giving Nourishment and Getting Interest

When I was a little girl I loved animals. Luckily, I grew up in the country and there was no shortage of wildlife around me. But I soon found out that most wild animals are skittish. If I walked right up and tried to pet them they immediately ran away. I realized quickly that if I wanted to form a relationship with the deer, squirrels, raccoons, and birds around my home I was going to have to come up with a way to attract them and then wait for these shy forest creatures to come to me.

Fortunately, I was not the only person in my house who had an interest in attracting wildlife. My grandmother showed me how to strategically place different kinds of food for the deer and squirrels, and how to put up a bird feeder and fill it with the things birds like. Soon I was able to quietly watch by the kitchen window early every morning as different animals showed up to sample what I had put out for them.

Something else happened that I hadn't anticipated. Yes, all sorts of animals did show up, but there were a few who became my best repeat customers. A big raccoon we named "Rocky" and a robin with a ragged wing whose name I can't remember now.

Rocky and Mr. Robin showed up the most. It was like they not only immediately loved the food I provided, but also decided to trust the source and add it to their list of "must-visit" places on spring mornings. A few times they brought friends too. And all the time I sat very still by the window and marveled at how awesome this whole experience was.

Now, as a grown woman who is a self-published author, I often think of Rocky and Mr. Robin and how much they taught me about marketing.

When I talk to my clients, or to random writers I meet on Twitter, or writers I run into at writing events, and I ask them all my standard marketing questions (the main one being, "How does the thought of marketing make you feel?") a common theme shows up again and again. So many of these writers tell me that they don't want to be pushy, they feel uncomfortable being aggressive, and they feel like the world of marketing will do the same thing the entire world has been doing to them since they were the shyest kid in the class in first grade: urge them to be more assertive.

I get it. About a thousand people during my lifetime have told me I should "be more assertive." Ironically enough, the moment I hear those words come out of their mouth I imagine punching them.

A lot of writers seem to picture marketing as a giant two-ton megaphone that they'll be handed unexpectedly. They'll have to balance the huge weight, while also climbing to the highest point possible, and then blast everyone below with a cheesy marketing message about how great they are and why everyone should read their book.

All I can say to that is, if I had used the megaphone strategy on the deer and squirrels and birds living in the fields around my farmhouse, how many of those animals do you think would have shown up in my front yard?

You got it.

I'm not saying the megaphone strategy doesn't have a time and place. If you're trying to market something to certain slices of the population it works very well—like rabid football fans on the day of the big game, or a bunch of drunk people at a packed pool party in Las Vegas. But that's NOT who you are trying to market to as a writer. You are trying to market to *readers*, and most readers are way more similar to the skittish deer and squirrels and birds I was trying to attract to my front yard.

The way I drew Rocky Raccoon and Mr. Robin to me is the same way you're going to draw readers to your writing work: You put out something good to eat, totally free of charge and easily accessible, and then you wait and watch to see who shows up.

Rocky Raccoon and Mr. Robin are your potential readers, obviously. Your website is the front yard. Google analytics (or any other easy way to track the traffic and clicks on your website) is the kitchen window you watch from to see who is showing up and if they're eating the food you put out. That just leaves one last piece, and it's maybe the most important piece of all—the food.

The food, or the "offering" you put out to attract potential readers, should be just that: a form of nourishment. Depending on what you write and what type of reader you're trying to attract, this form of nourishment might be different every time. In my case, I write articles about emotional issues that writers who are introverts and Highly Sensitive People deal with every day. The title of the article is the smell of food that attracts them, and then the information and insights offered in the article provide the nourishment. Once someone partakes of a few of my "nourishing" articles they know they can trust me as a source of good food. More often than not, they go on to buy my book, *The INFJ Writer*, because they already have a pretty good idea that the book will be just as nourishing too.

You can do something similar to this no matter what kind of writer you are. This is why offering a free chapter or a free excerpt of your novel on your website is such a good idea. For readers who love romance, a great love story nourishes their soul. For readers who are into mystery and suspense, the teaser of an enigma to be solved gets their mental gears going and promises the intellectual nourishment that comes from solving a difficult puzzle. For readers who are interested in seeing the world through the eyes of someone very different from them, an emotional chapter from a beautiful memoir lets them know they can find the experience they crave by giving the whole book a chance.

You can also do this by writing articles about the process of writing the book itself. Say, for example, you've written a book about your experience riding horses and how that experience has given you confidence and changed your life. Putting a blog post out there about a very personal incident that happened between you and your horse, and how that ignited something in you or made you see something about yourself, and how it also spurred you to write a book about your life with horses, is a great way to attract readers who will be interested in reading that book. The title and keywords of the article draw them in, the actual article nourishes them, and then the end of the article includes links to your book, showing them how they can receive more of this yummy food.

This can work particularly well for sci-fi and fantasy writers. I have one fantasy/horror writer friend who carefully details exactly how he went through his world-building process when writing his last book, and then includes links to the book on Amazon at the end of the blog post. I have another friend who writes fantasy fiction and writes different blog posts that concentrate on particular characters in the book, complete with the pictures of celebrities he would choose to play them if the book were turned into a movie. Blog posts like these are fun and interesting, and they provide food for the imagination. As a writer myself, I love to think about fantastical worlds and get to know new characters. The way these two writers share their process and their own vision of their characters is powerfully attractive to me.

So, okay, great, you've got some awesome ideas for the type of "food" you want to put out for readers and you've posted something up on your website. But…nothing's happening. Where are your readers? Where's Rocky Raccoon and Mr. Robin? Shouldn't they have shown up by now, and also brought some friends?

This brings us to another crucial point.

It's essential to put out good, nourishing food, but it's *also* essential to put it somewhere easily noticeable, easily accessible, and safe from predators.

Easily Noticeable

If you write one good blog post designed to attract readers and then it gets buried under a slew of other mundane updates, chances are slim that any first-time visitors to your website are going to dig through the pile to get to the one good blog post.

Super helpful tip: Create a "Best of" list of good blog posts and plant this in your sidebar big and bold so *any* visitor to your website can immediately see what they should be reading to get to the good stuff.

Easily Accessible

Okay, so your first potential Rocky Raccoon has spotted the food and is eating it, and *liking* it. Yay! But now, he wants to share it with his friends. The problem is, you put the food in kind of a weird place and it's a pain for Rocky to explain to everyone else how to get there. Wouldn't it be nice if there was a button he could push and all of his friends could instantly have access to this great food too?

Super helpful tip: This is the power of social media. We live in a world where there IS a button you can push and all of someone's friends instantly have access to the yummy food they've been ingesting online. It's called social media sharing buttons and they need to be at the end of *every single one of your blog posts*. Facebook and Twitter are essential, even if you don't use one or the other of these platforms yourself. Because even if you've sworn off Facebook or Twitter, other people haven't and they *do* use these things to share content with their people. Don't make them hunt for buttons or expect them to cut and paste your links. Make it as easy as it is to buy an e-book on Amazon with one click.

Safe from Predators

It might sound weird when I urge you to use moderation when marketing *anything* on your website, but that's exactly what I'm suggesting. If someone is attracted by the smell of food (the wonderfully clear, concise title of an article that draws them in on social media) and clicks on your link only to be immediately hit with a pop-up asking for their email address, and then after that various forms of you yelling at them to buy your book, or various forms of you trying to entice them to sign up for this or that thing you have going, they are probably going to see you more as a predator than a trustworthy source of good nourishing food.

Super helpful tip: Be mindful not only of what you want people to *do* when they get to your website, but also how you want them to *feel*. Think about all the places you visit online that offer you a form of creative nourishment. What do those people or websites do to make you feel safe and also interested in consuming more of what they have to offer?

Answer these quick questions to discover your own strategy of attracting Rocky Raccoon and Mr. Robin to your front yard:

Can you offer an excerpt of your book on your website?

Can you offer a free chapter?

Can you write a blog post about the hero of your story and what you love about him or her?

Can you write an article about a personal experience that inspired you to write your book?

Firefly Magic

Is there some part of your writing process you could share that might be interesting to other writers in your genre? (Remember, the other writers in your genre are also your readers.)

Does your book take place in a cool setting or time period that you could share details about?

Chapter 14

Creativity as Secret Weapon: Make More Things and Your Marketing Muscle Will Grow

The first weekend in May of 2017 I was on my way to Sedona, Arizona to teach at a writing retreat. I had flown into Phoenix Sky Harbor Airport and was now snugly settled on the shuttle bus that ran between Phoenix and Sedona, which was two hours away. My retreat happened to be at the Sedona Mago resort, which was even farther, located at the end of a long, winding, and extremely bumpy road. I was on one of the only shuttle buses that went to the resort. Since it was such a rough ride many others wouldn't do it.

We entered the city of Sedona and made stops here and there until I was the only one left on the bus. The driver had been wonderful the whole way so I decided to scoot up and sit closer to him as we made our way down the rutted dirt road to the resort.

The driver looked to be in his late 40s or early 50s. He had curly salt and pepper hair and a friendly gray beard. I asked him questions about the shuttle and he asked me questions about the retreat I was going to until we figured out that we were both artists of a sort, me a writer, and him a photographer.

"My husband's a photographer too!" I exclaimed and we were off and running from there. Like most photographers, this guy was enthusiastic about his art. He told me all about cool places he had been and amazing shots he had captured. It was obvious that photography was a lifelong passion for him.

"Wow," I said. "That all sounds so cool. Do you sell anything online?"

It was like I had doused him with a bucket of cold water.

My new friend immediately, and visibly, shut down. He hunched into himself, concentrated his eyes on the road and said politely (but still coldly) that he "hated all that marketing stuff."

This was when I really got interested. I had always been fascinated by limiting belief systems and how they worked inside of the human mind, and in the past year I had become almost obsessed with examining the limiting belief systems that most writers and artists hold about selling and marketing.

So, I asked him more questions.

I found out that this passionate photographer didn't even have a website. He had tried to put one up before, he said, but got too confused and frustrated by the whole process and gave up. He hated social media. It was impossible to make any money off photography these days anyway, he added.

I kept asking more questions.

It turned out that my new friend also used to be a teacher. He taught photography for a while at a community college and loved it, until he was laid off. He was also obsessed with media laws and the intricacies of copyright and trademarks on photography work. He was the president of a society that met every month to discuss and illuminate these obscure legal labyrinths.

The wheels in my head were turning so fast I swear smoke was coming out of my ears.

I started peppering him with ideas. Why didn't he put up a website, sell some of his images through Shutterstock, offer one-on-one coaching and photography workshops on the side, and throw together some quick-and-dirty legal tips in an e-book for aspiring photogs? He could have multiple streams of income, some of it passive, and also use his passion to inspire others in real time, out in the field.

I wish I could say my new friend loved my ideas and thanked me profusely. However, I think I just overwhelmed him. It was too much too fast and I was trying to dismantle limiting beliefs that had probably been in place for years, if not decades. No one can dissolve mental barriers like that in 20 minutes or less. Not unless powerful LSD is involved.

Since powerful LSD was not involved in this conversation with my shuttle driver, we didn't dissolve his limiting beliefs that day, and I'm guessing he probably still doesn't have a website up.

My shuttle driver is just one individual example, but he's a representative of the hundreds of writers and artists I meet every year who are struggling with the same limited mindset.

To the point: Most writers think that the only thing they can sell is books.

And yes, of course you want to sell books. All of us want to sell books. The selling of books should always be on your priority list. But, in this day and age of creative entrepreneurship, writers and artists are discovering they have so much more to offer than just the tangible pieces of their art. Also, because a lot of "business" these days pretty much means "online business" there are dozens of creative ways we can make multiple streams of income happen too.

Take the case of a writer I met at that same Sedona retreat I was just talking about. She had written a book and wanted to write more, but she also had a few other brilliant talents that she hadn't realized could be used to her advantage. She was extremely knowledgeable about gemstones and how certain gemstones could help with certain issues. I had just gotten into gemstones myself and had no idea where to start. There was so much information online and a lot of it was confusing or contradictory. When I said she could charge money in order for people to access her knowledge she was intrigued. When I suggested she could open up a stream of income by offering personal gemstone consultations, complete with a chart of customized recommendations for clients to take home, she was astonished.

Every writer I talk to—and I do mean *every* writer—is not *just* a writer. Each of us has other passions and hobbies and talents that we take for granted. To us, it's just stuff that interests us on the side, so how could it ever tie into our writing, or function as a business idea that might actually generate income? Who would pay us just because we happen to know a lot about a certain topic when anyone can access blogs, Youtube video tutorials, or plain old Google?

That's exactly it right there though. Anyone can access *literally millions of choices* through the internet to learn about something. When humans are confronted with that many choices, that is exactly when they need the most help.

Do you want to wade through a hundred results on Google to learn what you need to know about trademarking and copyrighting images? Or would you rather pay $3.00 for an e-book on quick-and-dirty legal tips that my shuttle bus driver has already put together for you?

Do you want to sift through dozens of different pages showing "gemstone properties," wasting time learning about countless gemstones that *don't* interest you while you find the one that does? Or would you rather pay to talk to a friendly woman on the phone for 30 minutes, describe your needs to her exactly, get informed recommendations, and then a follow-up email with a chart customized exactly for *you*?

This is how I generate the bulk of my coaching income. I help people make informed choices. Yes, as a writing coach I do actually help people with their writing. But more and more, writers aren't coming to me with writing problems, they're coming to me with choice problems. Should they self-publish or go traditional? That one question alone leads into mazes of other questions. They don't want to waste time following a choice that isn't the best fit for them. And most of them also suffer from the problem that is yet to be named in our society, but that we already definitely need a label for. How do you google the answer to something when you don't even know what it is you need to google?

Writers in the world today are not just writers anymore. That's the plain truth of it. We are all now creative entrepreneurs.

The type of online business model I'm talking about is called diversification, and it's exactly like diversifying the stocks in your investment portfolio. Smart investors know that the best way to strike a good balance between security and risk is to include various types of stocks and bonds in your portfolio, so if one company suddenly goes belly up, all your eggs aren't in that basket. It's exactly the same when it comes to your collection of online offerings. If you're *only* offering books, you're going to be hyper-focused on sales and numbers and probably driving yourself crazy trying to figure out how to sell more, more, more. This is exactly the place most creatives don't want to be in and why they tend to shy away from marketing and selling so much. They hate the pressure to sell more of their artistic work just to bring in material reward.

But, if a writer has diversified her online offerings and has a bad month in book sales, it's not as big of a deal. Not only on the money front, but also on the self-confidence, creative front. For instance, if you're a paranormal romance author who also offers online tarot readings on the side, and one month you hit a slump and sell no books, you can boost yourself back up by remembering that you did a great reading for one of your clients. You can focus on the fact that you helped that person. Moving back into the energy of service makes it so much easier to reassure yourself that your book sales will pick up in the future.

Okay, so you're on board with this whole diversification thing, but you don't know where to start. Here's a short list of online offerings from writers and artists that people are more than willing to pay for:

- *Short e-books on tips, tricks, and basic how-to methods*
- *One-on-one coaching sessions (writing, editing, public speaking, relationships, nutrition, astrology, divorce and fertility issues, and just about anything else)*
- *Consultant services (website/UX design, manuscript formatting, proofreading, book cover design)*
- *Images and illustrations*
- *Subscription services for daily or weekly video series that inform or teach about a creative topic*

You can also expand the collection of books you're offering for sale, without writing an entirely new novel. If you're a fantasy writer with a large cast of characters and a penchant for great worldbuilding, put out a companion encyclopedia that goes along with your book that includes all the background information and tiny little details about the characters and setting that you didn't have room for in the book. Years ago, I went through an Anne Rice phase and was more than happy to snap up the companion encyclopedia to her vampire series. I wanted to know every nitpicky little thing about Lestat and the encyclopedia delivered.

If you're a cozy mystery writer with a passion for food and travel, consider working in a bit of a culinary twist to your next novel, and then put out a companion collection of recipes that are recommended by the characters, or a regional travel guide with tourist spots they recommend. Again, years ago, I was a big soap opera fan, and when *Days of Our Lives* put out a cookbook with recipes "chosen" by the characters I snapped it up (and had a lot of fun trying them all out).

If you're a self-help author, think about putting out a companion workbook to go along with your latest book. Readers can read a chapter, and then turn to their workbook to do the exercises, or they can just use it as a journal as you encourage them to record their experiences and any revelations they might have while reading your book.

The possibilities are endless and the internet is expanding every day. For Highly Sensitive Writers, it's time to think bigger.

~

Try these exercises to start generating ideas for your own collection of diverse offerings, and your own multiple streams of income:

Write down the top three things you are interested in and passionate about outside of writing.

Now, devote a couple of paragraphs to each thing. Does this thing tie into your writing at all? Does it inspire your writing or is it the other way around? Is there no connection?

Spend a few minutes thinking about how you feel about teaching. Could you ever see yourself doing coaching sessions with people? What would that look like? Could you ever see yourself offering a workshop? What would that look like?

Make a list of "companion" books that could possibly go along with the book you're writing right now, or a book you've already finished. Make a check mark next to any that sound like they might be fun to explore.

Most importantly, keep thinking about it. The best ideas for new creative offerings tend to float into your mind when you're least expecting them.

Chapter 15

Start with the Symptoms: How to Sell Your Stuff to the People Who Actually Need It

I n May of 2015 I wrote a blog post called 'Writers of a Certain Age...Is It Too Late?' Over two years later I still get emails about that post. It also still brings me new clients, and they are always the type of clients I really love: writers who feel a deep soul calling to write and don't want to wait any longer to act on their dreams.

What's the secret of success behind my 'Writers of a Certain Age' post? Well, it's actually a simple formula that anyone can use to tap into the deepest needs of their audience.

But before we get to this magic formula, let's back up a minute and go over a few basics from Sales 101.

One of the first things anyone learns in sales is that selling things to people is about solving problems. After becoming a coach and selling coaching sessions to people, I wholeheartedly agree. Selling things *is* about solving problems. Every person who comes to you as a customer in any form—whether that's as a reader who might want to buy your book or a fellow writer who wants to hire you as an editor—is someone who needs your help to solve an issue in their life.

The tricky thing is that it's not always obvious what that problem or issue is. In fact, a lot of the time the customer himself doesn't even know he has the problem.

Good salespeople are the same as good business people. They have the insight and clarity to see how a partnership could benefit multiple parties. But *brilliant* salespeople are like great doctors. They have the empathy and listening skills to observe and ask questions to diagnose a set of symptoms, and they can then use that diagnosis to solve a problem the patient is suffering from, but also doesn't yet have a name for.

Let's go back to my 'Writers of a Certain Age' blog post to see how this works in action.

When I wrote that blog post two years ago, I already had a few years of experience in coaching frustrated writers. I had worked with many writers who had just turned 40, or were coming up on 50 or 60, and were in despair because they hadn't yet started the novel they had always dreamed of writing. I had seen the profile so many times that I knew it very well, and I also knew that there was a solution. I knew these writers didn't need to feel like a failure about their lives.

But, if I had written a blog post called, "If You're a Middle-Aged Writer Who Feels Like a Failure I Have the Solution for You!" I'm willing to bet that I would have gotten very little response. Because even if you ARE a middle-aged writer who feels like a failure, the chances are slim that you categorize yourself as that inside your own mind. Also, when it comes to dealing with emotional dissatisfaction in our lives, most of us don't examine our feelings and then come up with a label for the underlying problem that's causing the feelings. This is why we pay therapists large sums of money. Because that kind of thing is pretty difficult to do on your own.

So, if I had written a blog post that led with me stating the problem and then saying I had the solution, it would be the same as if I'd written an article called, "Do You Have the Rare Blood Disease XYZ? I Have the Solution for You!" Sure, there are a few people out there that know they have XYZ, but what about all the people who have it but don't know they have it? How can you help them if they don't even know that your solution is something they should be looking for?

That's where the magic formula comes in.

You always start with the symptoms, NOT the problem.

No matter how much information someone is lacking about the problem that's causing them pain and suffering, or just plain old dissatisfaction in their life (which, I would argue, is a form of pain and suffering), they *do* know how they feel. When you name the symptoms, and get really specific about them, it's like waving a red flag in front of your reader's face.

In the case of my blog post, I asked these questions to nail down the symptoms:

- *When you hear about the latest young writing phenom, do you bitterly note how old they are, and how much older you are than them?*
- *When you pick up the latest bestseller you've really been wanting to read, do you wonder what magical secret the author used to finish and publish such good work? Perhaps they were lucky, you might think.* Or have connections I could never hope to have.
- *Does the thought of your upcoming birthday—or even just the calendar year turning over—fill you with a feeling of frantic despair? Does your life feel like the hourglass is running out too fast?*

You can see how I concentrated on emotions in these questions. I used words like: "bitterly," "frantic," and "despair." I called up the image of an hourglass with sand running out of it. I painted a picture of someone picking up a bestselling book and the negative thoughts focused on comparison that might occur to them.

How did I decide to use these exact questions and images?

Easy. I just ransacked my own emotional closet.

This is the difference between heart powered marketing, and marketing to push a product. I didn't use the magic formula outlined above solely to get more clients. I didn't write that blog post just to get more traffic to my blog. The clients and traffic were nice, but the real reason behind it was my own experience, and the experiences other writers had shared with me. In fact, if you visit that blog post you'll see that I shared my own personal story, which was full of my own personal fears about being an aging writer.

I, too, have felt like a writer who is growing older and doesn't have anything to show for it. I, too, have felt like time is running out. I've *seen* that hourglass in my mind. I've picked up that best-seller and had those thoughts run through my head. I know how crappy it feels to go through it.

That's why I wanted to help other people who are currently going through the same thing.

But, you might be saying, *I write YA fantasy fiction about kings and warriors and pet dragons. How in the world am I supposed to use the "name-the-symptoms" formula in a blog post to bring in more readers?*

First, we start by digging into the core of your story. I don't care what you're writing about, if you're Highly Sensitive and you're a writer passionate about writing, the core of your story has some deeper meaning beyond the action and the plot. If you're writing middle grade or YA, it's very likely you're concerned with the process a person goes through to find their identity and their place in the world. Possibly you're interested in spreading the message of acceptance and diversity. If you're writing mystery/suspense you might be someone who values the intellect and the importance of initiative and self-reliance when it comes to figuring out problems in the world. If you're a romance writer, you might be pursuing what a love relationship looks like when both parties have true equality and are brave enough to be vulnerable with each other.

Once you have the idea or message that lies at the core of your story, you can start cooking. Ask yourself: Why is this idea or message so important to me? Is it because of some experience I had in the past that changed me or affected me deeply?

For me, I knew I wanted to write a blog post about writers turning 30, 40, and other milestone birthdays, and how that could bring up intense feelings of failure. But it wasn't until I sat with myself and tuned into my own heart, going over my own thoughts and memories about this issue, that I was able to name the symptoms of how it felt. That was when I was able to put my finger on the emotion words like, "bitter," and "frantic," and that was when I saw the image of the hourglass in my head, big as life.

That was when I was able to sit down and start writing that post from the heart.

This is how you can actually use a blog to market yourself as a writer. Now, I don't subscribe to the oft-repeated advice that *every* writer should have a blog. But, if you have one and you enjoy it then, yes, I do believe this is one of the best ways to use it. Explore your stories, find the messages at the core of them, examine how that's related to your own emotional baggage, and then write it all out in a blog post that will connect with readers who have similar issues.

As an example, your process might go something like this:

You've written a historical fiction novel about a woman who works as a prostitute in Victorian England.

You examine the core ideas and message behind your story: You care deeply about women's rights, you're fascinated with English culture in the Victorian era, and you also know what it's like to be judged for your choice of lifestyle.

You pick one message: women's rights.

You write a blog post opening with a personal story: your first experience of realizing that men and women receive different treatment and the sense of outrage you felt at the time. You follow with questions for your reader: have they experienced these feelings or thoughts about feminism, women's history, or current politics? You end by dovetailing into a brief summary of your book and how it's related to the themes and ideas you've just outlined. You provide specific links on where to get the book and encouragement to leave their opinions about these topics in the comments below.

A few weeks later you can write another blog post using theme number two (fascination with English culture in the Victorian era) and then a few weeks later repeat it again with theme number three (being judged for choice of lifestyle).

By examining our own beliefs and the ideas at the core of our work, and then sharing that intimate knowledge with others, we show readers why we wrote the book we did, and why they should care. We reveal how our book could contribute to their own store of knowledge, or emotional balance and health.

We let them know that we are a kindred spirit, and we open the door to potentially positive relationships with people who are on the same wavelength as us.

Try using these questions to get at the core message of your story:

What is most important to the hero of your story?

Why do you think the villain of your story is dangerous? Why should they be stopped?

What character traits have made your hero successful as a person?

Do you see any archetypes showing up in your stories that you personally identify with? Do you tend to write about Damsels-in-Distress or Orphan Children? Do your villains all tend to be Gamblers or Addicts? What are these archetypes trying to tell you?

Firefly Magic

Is there a difficult life experience you've gone through that keeps showing up in your work? Do you think your experience with this difficult event could be of help to others in some way? How did you specifically, emotionally feel when you were going through it? Make a list of symptoms.

Chapter 16
Deep Listening: Why Highly Sensitive Writers Make the Best Salespeople

F rom the first day I started my coaching business I have offered what is known as the "free consultation." The free consultation is a technique (or tactic, depending on how you look at it) used by many different companies and salespeople to draw in new customers, hoping to get them to sign up for continued services. I have never used it like that. Instead, before every one of my free consultations I sit quietly for a few minutes and offer up this prayer:

"Universe, you have sent this person to talk to me for some reason. Please help me to serve their highest good in whatever way I possibly can at this time."

This dramatically shifts the interaction in a more positive way and, I would say, increases the potential for creative problem-solving at least tenfold. Any expectations I might have about gaining a client are instantly dropped, leaving me free and clear to actually help the person and learn something myself in the process. Always a win-win. I have also found that if I am meant to work with the person, it will happen. I don't need to "do" anything special during the consultation because, if it's meant to be, the

Universe will make it abundantly clear that a coaching relationship is in the best interest of both of us.

But what this also means is that I talk to a lot of people on the phone who *don't* end up becoming clients. During our conversation I usually get nudges and signs that a coach is not what they need at this time and their highest good would be better served by a different option for growth. However, I have never, ever left a free consultation without feeling that I did help the person in some way, and it was still a win-win for both of us.

I have talked to a mother who lost an adult child to suicide, a spoken-word poet who realized she wanted to pursue acting lessons, stay-at-home moms who decided they wanted to go back to school, and a whole long list of people who just needed a push to set aside one hour a week for their writing. I have listened while total strangers have cried, broken down, ranted, questioned, and worked through blocked energy during a free consultation. When I tell people about these emotional phone calls that don't pan out into a new client sign-up, I always get the confused look. "Isn't that frustrating?" People have asked me. "You're not even getting paid."

First of all, the free consultation is not about getting paid. And second, I am receiving something way more valuable than money.

These people are sharing themselves with me.

The writers who call me for free consultations but never become clients are giving me a very personal glimpse into their lives, their hearts, and their minds. They are sharing with me honestly what they are afraid of, what motivates them, all that they hope for, and all of their dreams.

In case you didn't know, I'm a blogger who writes about writing, creativity, personality, and life inspiration. I also write books that fall into the self-help, personal growth category.

So, people opening their hearts and sharing what makes them blossom and what shuts them down, to me, is more valuable than gold.

These free consultations that don't end up as new clients still feed *my* inspiration. They give me dozens of clues—neon signs, if you will—pointing me toward where I need to go. They show me what the next blog post I write should be about, and what the next topic of my latest book should concentrate on. They show me where people are hurting, and what the world needs the most from my creative talents right now.

When I started chewing my way through a long list of selling and marketing books last year to do the research for this book, I found that salespeople across the board had already discovered this very same thing. In fact, it seems that "empathy skills" have been making a slow but steady rise in the arsenal of tools recommended to salespeople since the 1980s. Eric Baron talks about "consultative selling" in *Selling Is a Team Sport*, and Michael Bosworth and John Holland emphasize superb listening skills as a top predictor of sales success in *CustomerCentric Selling*. Over and over again, I saw the same approach recommended by a variety of different sales methodologies: slow down, listen to what the other person is actually trying to tell you, and then, if you can, genuinely try to help them.

For Highly Sensitive Writers, this is what we've been doing our entire lives as a natural tendency of our inborn temperament.

However, because of the "way I am" as a Highly Sensitive Person, I always assumed that meant I would be a disaster at sales and marketing. I assumed that my empathy work with total strangers during free consultation calls was probably something no good business person would indulge in. I wasn't making any money as a result of these calls—and wasn't that what salespeople and marketers were single-mindedly focused on? Making money at the expense of people?

Imagine my astonishment when I found out how very wrong I was on that.

As I read sales book after sales book, from the 1950s to the present day, from Napoleon Hill to Guy Kawasaki, the evidence mounted until I couldn't deny it anymore. My stereotypical beliefs about sales and marketing people were shattered.

Book after book said the same thing: If you push things on people who don't want or need those things, you won't get very far. A good salesperson has integrity of character and seeks to actively help people by selling them a product that will make their lives better.

A few books even urged the salesperson to walk away from the sale if they determined that what they were selling was not the right fit for the customer.

My mind was blown.

According to my worldview, I was an artist. I was a writer, kind of a hippie, a free spirit, and a conscious, compassionate person. I valued growth, inclusion, fairness, and diversity. Sales and marketing people were aggressive, competitive, and only out for themselves.

But it turns out that the method I was using naturally in my free consultation calls, which also brought creative inspiration for my own work, and many times a new long-lasting client, was the very same method being espoused in the top sales books over the last three decades.

I have never met a writer who didn't care about her audience. I have never met a writer who didn't think about what kinds of people might read his stories. I have never met a writer who didn't obsess over this or that detail in her manuscript and how it would affect the reader on the other end.

Any writer who has even done two minutes of marketing research has seen the oft-touted advice: Find where your audience hangs out and then hang out there too. Sometimes this is easy. If you write superhero-style stories you're definitely going to want to visit at least one of the many different comic cons that happen every year around the country. But what if you write steampunk middle grade fiction? Or time travel erotic fiction with a reincarnation theme? It's not so easy to immediately determine where these kinds of readers are clustered and go directly to them.

And this is where those empathy skills we were just talking about come in.

When you develop your empathy skills, you can start generating creative, alternative ideas on how to reach your readers. When you consistently practice listening to people, like I was doing in all of those free consultation calls, you start hearing what people are trying to tell you, you start connecting the dots on where your people are and what they might be looking for.

Empathy skills are made up of a two-part process: listening and imagining. First, you actively listen to a bunch of people, making no judgments about their opinions or suggestions, just taking it all in. Then, you go inward to sift through all that information and imagine what you need to know about your potential audience: where do they buy their books, how do they find new books to read, and what would interest them the most. You put yourself in their shoes. If you were a seventh-grade girl who likes magic, horses, and space travel, how would you get your hands on a new book? Hmmm...that leads us to this girl's parents. Okay, if you were the parent of a girl who likes magic, horses, and space travel, what would catch your eye about a book and make you consider buying it for your daughter?

Effective brainstorming, brilliant inspiration, creative marketing strategy, and powerful selling are all turbo-charged when you add empathy skills and imagination to the mix.

Highly Sensitive Writers are born with these skills. In fact, we have them in much higher proportion than the rest of the population. The elements of your personality that have always made you feel like you were "too sensitive" or "too weird" or that you need to get your "head out of the clouds" are the very same kind of talents that make great marketing and sales teams shine. It's just that most Highly Sensitive Writers never discover this. They're stuck in old, outdated belief systems about themselves and assume that they can never be good at sales or marketing.

Yes, sales and marketing in the 1960s might have been all about slippery manipulation tactics—Don Draper in Mad Men being a very good example. But in our current day, where everyone lives their lives half in the real world and half online, those slippery tactics don't fly anymore. There is just too much information readily available for free and at our fingertips. If someone is too pushy or isn't genuinely interested in their customers, it's way too easy to find ten bad reviews that attest to the fact and that will steer the potential audience elsewhere.

Highly Sensitive Writers have the clear advantage. Not only do we care about our readers, we ARE our readers. There is nothing we want more than to inspire them, wow them, soothe them, and help them grow.

This is why I believe that THE BEST sales and marketing people could very possibly be Highly Sensitive Writers. Because we don't have to attend a sales training program to learn what we already do naturally. We don't have to conduct customer surveys to figure out what we should make more of and who might be interested in the things we're already making. We already are insanely curious about people, what drives them, what inspires them, and what makes their hearts break over and over again.

We already possess the skill set of the very best marketing gurus out there.

It's just a matter of realizing how good we could be at this, and then giving ourselves permission to get even better.

$$\sim$$

Try the following exercises to dig deep into your belief systems about marketing, and to see if you can replace any outdated beliefs with a new perspective:

Quickly write down the top ten words that you associate with the word "sales," "salesperson," or "selling."

Quickly write down the top ten words that you associate with the word "marketing."

Look at all the words you wrote down and now divide them into a "negative" column and a "positive" column. Read the words in the negative column carefully.

Now think about these people: Oprah Winfrey, Marianne Williamson, Elizabeth Gilbert, and Cheryl Strayed. What do they all have in common? Each one of them is brilliant at sales and marketing and embraces it.

Look at your column of negative words again. Would you use any of these negative words to describe the women above? Why or why not? Do you still believe your list of negative words is entirely accurate?

Chapter 17
"Contagious" Is a Good Thing: How to Price Your Work So That It Sells

One of my writer friends recently came out with a book and I was super excited to read it. I had enjoyed reading her blog for quite a while, and so I knew I would probably like her stories too. On publication day I eagerly clicked over to Amazon to buy the book and found...that paperback copies were listed at $16.99. Ouch. *Okay, no problem,* I said to myself. I'd pick up the Kindle copy instead. I clicked over again and found the e-book selling for...$9.99. Geez. I was really disappointed.

This lady was a self-published author just like I was, so I knew that she could set her own prices. Of course, printing costs always factor in somewhere, but I also knew that if a book didn't run into a crazy high word count you could rely on being able to price the print copy somewhere between $7.99 to $9.99. E-books had no printing costs at all, so there was never a reason to run above that $2.99 sweet spot.

I wanted to support my writer friend but $16.99 looked to my brain like a round $17, and $17 looked like "almost 20." I'm not saying these assumptions were accurate, I'm just telling the truth about where my brain went with these figures and how the psychological *feeling* I had about the prices influenced me to switch this book from "I'm-buying-it-today" to "I'll-buy-it-someday."

Well, I did buy it someday (like I said, I wanted to support my friend). But, it was months later when I felt like I had some extra cash to splurge on purchases. Then it took me another two months to get to the book in my to-be-read pile. So when it was all said and done, I ended up leaving a stellar review of my friend's book almost a year after her book launch.

Also, at $16.99 I wasn't buying her book as a gift for any of my friends, all of who are bookworms themselves.

What happened here?

There are dozens of books and blog posts out there on pricing strategy in general, and book pricing specifically. There are many experts who will tell you that $.99 to $2.99 is always the sweet spot to price an e-book for any emerging author, and that the higher you price any kind of copy of your book, the less likely it is that readers will give it a try if they've never heard of you before. In my opinion, this is all true.

But, there are another couple of things going on here that are also helpful to explore.

One is the psychological *feeling* we get about price. Again, there are tons of experts who will tell you that buying decisions are always based on emotion, even though we mainly think we base them on logic. I believe this is true too. I also believe that when you're a voracious consumer of anything over a long period of time, you get used to a certain set of feelings around the price of that thing that act as a kind of inner emotional thermostat.

Me, I'm a book hound. I worked for four years at a used bookstore chain. I read an average of 80 books a year (not joking) and I send every book I read to a prison donation program to make room for more. I go to massive annual sales for three different libraries every year. I live in San Francisco and frequent no less than five exquisite little used bookstores. I get free promo copies from authors and I have numerous bookworm friends who are always sending me books that they say are utterly fantastic.

I'm used to paying an average of $3.00 for a book, any book.

I get lots of free books from one channel or another.

I have a bottomless to-be-read pile.

So, paying $16.99 for a book just feels *weird* to me.

This is the first thing to consider when you start seriously thinking about how you want to price your book. If you are an emerging author, an indie author, or an author who is not J.K. Rowling or Stephen King (so that's pretty much all of us) you have to be very aware of the price spectrum and how pricing your books on the low end can actually help you out much more in the long run.

Of course, I'm speaking for self-published authors here. If you're signed with a traditional publisher they call the shots on pricing and that's that.

So that's the first "money thing" to consider when it comes to getting your book out there. The second is your marketing budget and how you want to invest your advertising dollars. A lot of authors put aside money for advertising and promotion and spend it all on advertising. That is, they take out expensive ads online, or sink every dollar into Kindle promo newsletter services. Very few authors who are new to the game set aside a significant amount of money to buy their own discount copies of their book.

If you are self-publishing, you can order your own discounted copies directly from the CreateSpace dashboard, or directly from whatever print-on-demand service you may be using. If you're with a hybrid publisher or a traditional publisher, you should also be able to receive discounted copies. Check your contract to see what your discount is. In the case of self-publishing, all of that will be transparent once you login to your account and order a copy.

What are you going to do with all these discounted copies that you're ordering for your own use?

These are your promo copies. You're going to give them away.

This is also where we might run into the same mental obstacle that was responsible for my writer friend pricing her debut novel at $16.99.

I'm going to say something here that might bring up immediate resistance in you. That's okay. Just keep reading and I'll explain more as we go. Here it is:

You are not in this writing game to make an income from it, at least not at first. As a new or just-getting-rolling author, the more you concentrate on making money from your books, the less copies of your books will end up in the hands of readers.

That means, if you have the choice to price a book high and make more dollars on every sale, or price a book low and get more readers overall, you must shift out of the get-money mindset and price low.

It also means, if you can save money by not ordering any promo copies, or spend money by ordering a bunch and distributing them throughout your grassroots community, you must shift out of the save-money mindset and distribute.

Here's the thing: a paper copy of a book is like a virus. A good virus. It can sit somewhere basically *forever* and wait to be opened. It can travel in suitcases, backpacks, purses, and diaper bags. It can get left behind on airplanes, in coffee shops, and at travel rest stops. It never expires. It is always waiting to be discovered.

Here's the other thing: there is a certain type of person out there who was infected with this book virus long ago and is now more than happy to spread it around wherever they can. These people sniff out garage sales and strangers' bookshelves. They pick through discarded paperbacks they find on the street. When they find a book they like they give or recommend it to an average of five people. Those five people pass it on to their own circles of five people. The ripples never end.

Do you see the pattern here?

The more copies of your book that you can get into the hands of these book virus carriers, the more successful your book will be.

The lower your book is priced, and the more free copies you can give away, the better your chances are of spreading your own book virus.

As someone who should be almost single-mindedly focused on spreading your book virus, you simply cannot work within the mindset of withholding—which is what most of the "get money" and "save money" energy is at the core. Yes, I do understand that *eventually* you would like to make money doing this writing thing. I totally get that. And if you're already making thousands of dollars each month in royalties or it doesn't seem that farfetched that Oprah might read your book this year, then disregard everything I'm saying.

But, if you're like me, a writer who is also an entrepreneur, who is also a mom, who is also still working a day job, and you could use all the readers you can get, then your best bet is going to be shifting out of withholding and shifting into give-give-GIVE. Because your best marketing tools are your works. Every single book you have written and published is a shiny, gorgeous, informative packet of marketing materials that showcases you and your talent.

Here's a third thing for you to chew on: Most people think that marketing is made up of a bunch of skills that help you push your products onto other people. But this is the truth: Marketing does not have to be only a skill set that helps you to get other people to buy your stuff. *Marketing can also be a value mindset* that helps you become open to and actively interested in participating in an ongoing service of exchange with your community.

Almost every "best book I have ever read" seemed to drop out of the sky into my lap. A friend sent me a copy or the cover attracted me and it was only $1.00 at a book sale. Or someone shared a link on Twitter and I clicked over and found the e-book was only $1.99 and what did I really have to lose? Book people are like this. We take chances. We share what we like and we talk about it, profusely.

Put your book somewhere easy to find and make it easy to get and it will more than likely fall into the right hands.

This exercise comes from one of my own personal marketing strategies. It takes some time and bit of work, but it's extremely rewarding in the "giving back to your community" department:

One of my favorite things to do is to give away copies of my books to Little Free Libraries. If you haven't heard, Little Free Libraries are boxes filled with books (usually built in the shape of little houses and painted in bright cheerful colors) that are set up by people near their house or place of business, and that operate on the take-a-book-leave-a-book system. In the past few years they've popped up all over the place in urban areas all over the world. In my experience, Little Free Library Stewards take their roles very seriously and are always delighted to receive new books to add to their collection.

First, take a look at the Little Free Library map at: https://littlefreelibrary.org/ourmap/

Enter your own zip code first and see if there are any Little Free Libraries in your area.

Then, check any other cities you feel connected to—it might be somewhere you used to live, or even the setting of the novel you're trying to market.

Now, hover over different map pins on the map. See how boxes of information come up that show you the address of the library and who owns it? As you hover and explore you'll notice that some boxes have more info than others, and that some owners have included what kinds of books they keep stocked or why they wanted to add a library to their neighborhood.

Start a list. Look for people who have included an email address for their Little Free Library and add them. When you have a list of about ten people, write a quick form letter that you can personalize on the fly and start contacting people. Ask each library steward if they would be open to you sending them a copy of your book to add to their Little Free Library.

Some people will answer you and some people won't. It doesn't matter how many responses of "yes" you receive though, there are always more Little Free Libraries to contact. You can also drive around your local area and deposit copies of your book into any Little Free Libraries you find near your neighborhood.

This is one strategy to help you spread the good virus of your book. You give back to your book community (even if it's across the country), you can plant copies of your book in far-flung places, and each copy will be in a place guaranteed to draw eclectic book-worms just waiting to give a new book a chance.

Chapter 18
It's Not 1985 Anymore: How Micro Niches Changed the World

I grew up in a small, somewhat rural, town in Michigan in the 1980s. We had one movie theater that was sometimes open, and sometimes closed for months. We had one Kmart, and one McDonald's and one Burger King, all out by the highway. My family had one television that got four channels.

Obviously, there was no internet.

Back in those days brand loyalty was a big thing. There were McDonald's people and Burger King people. There were Pepsi people and Coke people. My family was a McDonald's and Coke family, although I knew Burger King and Pepsi people too. I remember one friend of the family who would come over to spend the day with us and bring her own two-liter of Pepsi because she knew we would only have Coke in the house.

For those of us who grew up in the 70s and 80s, or in the decades before, with no internet, we remember those days well. Advertisers competed fiercely to win your loyalty, because once they "won you" you were very likely a customer for life. Even if that meant lugging your own two-liter of soda around with you just to make sure you stuck with the brand you liked.

The act of buying and selling, and the psychology behind

buying and selling, operated like this for so long that for those of us born pre-1990 this seemed like the way of the world, a way that would never change. The reality of there being two top brands at each other's throats to sell their product to the majority of the market, and then maybe a third underdog runner up (think RC Cola or Wendy's) was so all pervasive, so much the only thing most of us in the modern world had ever known, that we didn't question it. This was the way buying and selling worked.

I remember, growing up in the 80s, how difficult and magical it was to come across some sort of musical or artistic outlier. I remember very well my first boyfriend loaning me a cassette tape of a Rush album he had tape recorded from someone else and how lucky I felt to be able to borrow it for a whole week. I remember staying up late one night and seeing Morrissey perform on Saturday Night Live in a gold lamé shirt, tossing the microphone cord around like it was a snake on fire and being absolutely entranced. Who was this strange man? I was a 12-year-old girl with cows for next door neighbors on one side and cornfields on the other, and did I mention we only got four channels on our TV? Morrissey hit me like a bolt of lightning.

I also remember stumbling upon an old dog-eared copy of *Waiting for Godot* way down at the bottom of the shelves in one of my English classes. I remember pulling it out, reading a few pages, and looking at the impossibly craggy embittered face of Samuel Beckett on the back. His face looked like a mountain, a bitter mountain, and I knew that I was in love.

Back before the internet, these moments of discovery and magic were all a weirdo sensitive kid had sometimes.

Since then though, the world has radically changed. Like many others, I don't believe the human race will even grasp the depth of the changes the internet has brought to our civilization until a hundred years or so has passed, maybe even more, and we can see the ripple effect in its entirety. But what I do know now is that the days of Coke vs. Pepsi and McDonald's vs. Burger King are gone.

The world in which you only had a handful of choices, and a limited amount of shelf space to store the physical objects you needed to hold media, is gone too.

And even if some of the big publishers still don't get that, I'm seeing more and more that with every passing day, the writers and artists *do*.

I think this might be why so many of us who are in the older generations (and by older, I mean over 30) get a little tangled up in our thought processes about marketing. Some part of our brain is still stuck in the Coke vs. Pepsi days. When we imagine marketing our YA fantasy novel we imagine that we'll be competing with Harry Potter and Veronica Roth's *Divergent*. When we think about who might want to read our memoir we become discouraged because Cheryl Strayed's *Wild* was so damn good we doubt we could compete with that. But thinking in terms of competing with these mega-bestsellers is using an outdated mode of thought.

The current truth is: Readers aren't struggling to make room using finite shelf space in their homes anymore. They have infinite space available to them on their Kindles.

The eternal truth is: Voracious readers always want to explore and discover new books and new writers. They have never found one author, or even a handful of authors, and taken a lifelong vow to read those authors' books and nothing outside of that.

In this intense new online world that we all live in, marketing is no longer about blanketing the entire population with your advertising message. It is no longer about trying to convince poten-tial readers that you're "better" than another choice or "the best" choice they could make. It's no longer about persuading someone to "pick you" over someone else.

In a land where there are thousands of books for only 99 cents, unlimited space in which to store them, and readers who are getting ever-more-savvy at searching for specifics, everything is actually on your side marketing-wise.

This is usually when I hear the same old argument from writers.

But, if there are a million choices, isn't that bad for me? Won't I need to work harder to even get noticed? Won't the competition be that much more fierce?

If we're using the Coke vs. Pepsi mindset then the answer to those questions is a resounding yes. But we don't live in that world anymore. We now live in a new world, a world full of possibilities, opportunities, and micro niches.

Chris Anderson talks about this idea at length in *The Long Tail*, a stunning examination of the way the economy and what is on offer to buy and sell has changed as a result of the internet. Anderson explains that instead of the corporate giants only offering us "the hits" (blockbuster movies and NYT bestselling books), the internet gives us a vast wealth of choices that trickle into what is called "micro niches." The really cool thing, and what Anderson explores throughout the book, is that each of these micro niches has an audience all its own.

I've seen this myself in the writing world. I've stumbled across people writing Amish sci-fi and leprechaun erotica. Just the other day I found a pop-up book about vaginas and periods on Twitter. These are some of the more extreme "weird" topics and genres I've seen, but they are by no means the only ones. You can bet that the artists behind these kinds of works are not invested in the Coke vs. Pepsi mindset, because if they were, they wouldn't get anywhere.

As a writer working with micro niches you don't need to "capture market share" and you don't need to duke it out with Harry Potter. You just need to state what you're offering clearly, in a way that will reach people who might be potentially interested in checking it out.

So, for example, say you're writing a YA time travel romance featuring a female protagonist who cuts herself. In the old, outdated Coke vs. Pepsi mindset you would want to blast all your social media channels with a sizzling ad campaign for your book and talk about how it's the best YA romance of the year. You would want to pay exorbitant sums for advertising that shows why your story is more compelling than any other story. Your goal would be for a million YA romance fans to instantly recognize the title of your book, and ideally, to have bought it, read it, reviewed it, and recommended it.

Wow. That's a ton of expectation. No wonder most writers feel overwhelmed when they think of "competing" with everything else out there.

In the new world of micro niches, you don't need to compete. You just need to be clear about what you're offering and have some ideas about who might be interested in it or benefit from it. So, using the YA romance example above, let's say you've decided to approach your marketing with possible micro niches in mind. So, you start a blog where you talk about your writing process, and the issue of teen self-harm. You post links to helpful resources and also write and post articles about your experience of writing a socially-conscious YA novel. You add a video page that links to your Youtube channel where you post videos of you talking about your heroine and what inspired you to write her into being, and also interviewing other YA authors about socially-conscious YA topics that mean a lot to them. You make a Facebook page for YA time travel fans and start following people on Twitter who are into romantic fantasy, time travel, YA books, and mental health awareness.

Then, you make sure you have relevant keywords attached to everything—obvious words like "romance" and "time travel," but also less obvious terms like "teen cutting" and "mental health stigma" to make it more likely that people will find you when they're using Google to explore options. As you do all of this you realize you're having a whole lot of fun.

That's the reality of today's kind of marketing. You're not trying to push your thing onto a whole bunch of people who may or may not want it, or whose best interest it might serve, or it might decidedly not. Instead, you're exploring and connecting. You're making things that feel right to you and sharing them online. You're reaching out to other people who like the same kinds of things. You're saying, "Hey, I write YA romance with a time travel twist that features a heroine who cuts herself. Interested?"

You don't have to have a business degree. You don't have to be competitive, or aggressive, or be good at practical tasks. You just have to be you and find a way to authentically represent what kind of things you make and why people might like them. And I can already hear some of you saying, "But what if *no one* likes my things?" That's the power of micro niches though, there is someone for everyone.

You have to trust that readers know what they're doing and give them more credit. Just because someone is confronted with a million choices for books on Amazon doesn't mean that they won't be interested in yours. It also doesn't mean that you have to do virtual cartwheels and handstands to get them to notice you. It really is usually a matter of thinking carefully about what kinds of keywords you want to use when describing your book. For instance, you can bet the person writing leprechaun erotica isn't settling for plain old "fiction" or "fantasy." That person needs to be authentic, and specific, about exactly what they're selling.

You do too.

∽

Consider these questions to get you started on drilling down into how micro niches might apply to your writing:

What broad genre would you say your book is in? Romance? Mystery? Contemporary fiction?

What are some of the more specific genres your book might fall into? Is it middle grade high fantasy or new adult paranormal fantasy? Sweet romance or sexy thriller? Jump on Google for a minute and research all the subgenres of your broad genre.

Now think about some of the themes your book deals with that are personal to you and your work. Does your hero struggle against bullies? Does substance abuse or addiction make an appearance? Do any of your characters struggle against circumstances related to their ethnic identity or sexual orientation?

Is there anything that you feel is "weird" about your story or not like anything you've seen anywhere else? Many times, the elements in our book that resist categorization or give us a headache when it comes to placing them squarely in a genre can be a hidden blessing. Those are the elements that set our book apart and point us most promisingly toward a micro niche.

Make a list of words that describe your book, including the broadest and the most specific. Then, plug those words into Google and see what comes up. Plug them into Twitter as well and see if you can find anything there. Who else is talking about this stuff? Who else is interested? Make a note of it.

Chapter 19
No Writer Is a Marketing Island: Building Your Dream Team

I was just finishing up a consultation call with a new client and feeling super excited about working together. We had instantly clicked. Her book sounded amazing and I couldn't wait to read it. Also, I was in awe of what a brave person she was. Her memoir was all about events that had happened to her family, some of them so high-profile that the story made national news at the time. I was more than a little intrigued and very impressed with this woman's courage in moving forward and writing a book that would no doubt bring even more controversy into her life.

Then she said something that I never forgot.

"I'm so grateful to have you on the team, Lauren."

The team? I was confused. I asked for details.

"Well," she chuckled. "Ever since I knew I was serious about pursuing this project I started making plans to assemble my dream team. That was over a year ago. Since then I found a book cover designer whose work I'm in love with, a marketing coach who I know will be compassionate about the subject matter but also effective in helping me to get the story out there, and you—my ideal editor. You guys are my dream team. I know I can't possibly go wrong with all of you in my corner."

Wow. I loved that idea.

I thought about that conversation for the next week. My new client was definitely onto something with that, something big.

Another couple of weeks passed and I had a call with another client. This writer was a romance author who worked with LGBTQA themes in her novels. At the time of our call she was panicking because she had invested money in online advertisement space months ago, but she still didn't have the images she needed for the ad. "I'm no graphic designer," she told me hurriedly. "And this ad needs to look professional. But I just don't have the time to figure out how to do it and make it actually look good."

Had she checked out Fiverr? I asked. I'm sure she could find someone there in just a couple of minutes who could do exactly the thing she needed, and for a low price too.

What's Fiverr? she said.

And another light bulb went off in my head.

I've worked with dozens of writers who are trying to go it alone, and struggling mightily, myself included. Many of us put off dealing with our website issues for months—or even getting one up in the first place—because we aren't technical people and the thought of trying to figure it out is just too overwhelming. Some of us hire someone to design and implement a website for us, but then we feel like the job order is done and we can't ask questions months later or request ongoing issues to be fixed, so we end up neglecting our websites again.

A lot of writers I've met have tried to design their own book covers, and suffered through weeks of hair-pulling frustration as they try to nail down the specs they need for the e-book and the paperback version, and how to make everything fit together. More than a few writers have emailed me from the depths of what they almost universally refer to as "formatting hell," that agonizing process of making sure every line goes where it's supposed to in both the Kindle version and the hard copy.

And then there are those writers who hate marketing, and really can't overcome it. For whatever reason, learning about marketing is just not ever going to be anything they can dive into without gritting their teeth and growing resentful over the number of writing hours they might be losing to promotional work.

As I looked closer I saw the giant hairy problem that was blocking all of us, and how my new client who had built her "dream team" had so effectively untangled it, and then moved beyond it.

So, my new question was, why weren't more writers building their own "dream teams"?

The answer was in that second coaching call I'd had, with my client who didn't know about Fiverr.

It seemed that a lot of us, myself included, were so busy trying to fit creativity and writing into an already packed life filled with day jobs and spouses and children and other life activities, that we hadn't had the time to look around and see all the infinite choices for support available to us.

To be fair, all these choices are also a very recent development that has come about as a direct result of the self-publishing revolution. I'll say that again, because it's extremely important. What's happening today with self-publishing is nothing short of a *revolution*. It is on the scale of an earthquake and a volcanic eruption happening all at once in terms of the tools that writers now have available to them. Along with this huge shift, a number of various symbiotic relationships have sprung up. Because if you add new forms of life to any ecological system, other new forms of life will evolve to work together with them in new relationships.

The same thing is now happening for writers. There are millions of support people out there who are looking to enter into a symbiotic relationship with authors. Freelance editors, formatters, graphic designers, web designers, book cover designers, social media marketers, PR people, and coaches of all stripes have grown out of the self-publishing revolution, and they have just the skills and abilities we need to help us become successful writers.

Too many writers are trying to be a one-man or one-woman show when it comes to this whole writing business. Embracing yourself as an entrepreneur is essential, yes, but the lone wolf mentality isn't going to get you very far. If you really want to go places with your writing, you need to put together a dream team just like my client did.

But aren't some writers already doing that? You might be wondering. *Hiring random people off the internet isn't exactly a radical idea.*

I'm not talking about hiring random people off the internet though. I'm talking about building a dream team. Hiring random people to complete one-off tasks is like buying cheap IKEA furniture that falls apart in a few years. Adding valuable players to your dream team is like investing in good solid furniture that you can pass down for generations.

Your dream team should be made up of people that you respect, like, and deeply trust. That means your website guy (or lady) should be someone you can turn to with issues on an *ongoing* basis, and someone who is willing to take the time to explain to you what's included in their pricing. Your book cover designer should be someone who genuinely listens to your vision and works with you to make it come to life. If you hire a marketing coach, that person should be someone who is interested in working with you at your pace, and honoring the intention you want to put behind your marketing message to the world.

This is not to say that you can't find someone good off a website like Fiverr, because you most definitely can. But it is a reminder to be thoughtful and careful when you choose the people you want to add to your dream team. Your dream team people are ideally going to be support people who you will work with for *years*, so the quality of relationship you build with them is going to be very important.

Every author's dream team will be different. Yours should be a small community of people who fit your unique needs as a writer, whatever those might be. So, that might mean that you don't have a book cover designer on your team, whether it's because you've gone the traditional publishing route so you don't need one, or because you're also a visual artist and designing your own cover is a deliciously fun task for you and you would never want to give it up. It might mean that you don't need a website person, because you've already held a few different positions in your day-job life as an IT tech and you would rather cover that part of the process yourself.

To give you an example of a dream team at play, here are the support people I currently have in place that I couldn't imagine moving forward without:

Formatter

My formatter is a ROCK STAR. I can't even remember how I found her, but I'm never letting her go. Whenever I have a final draft ready of my manuscript I send it off to her for Kindle format-ting (e-book), and CreateSpace (print copy). She has gone back and forth with me countless times when I want the chapters head-ings to "just look this certain way" or when I can't figure out why an extra page keeps showing up in CreateSpace but not in the Word doc. I've had projects where I've sent her no less than 30 to 40 emails trying to get things just right and she is always calm, gentle, and extremely clear in helping me get where I need to be. This woman has the patience of a saint and the cheerful good humor of a Zen master. I can't even tell you how many times she's brought me back from the brink during the self-publishing process.

Book Cover Designer

I started out with a book cover designer that I liked for my first book, but then for my second book I got stuck. This wasn't my book cover designer's fault. They offered a basic kind of service and I needed something much more in depth. The problem was that I sort of knew what I wanted, but didn't really know what I wanted at all. I needed someone to talk it through with me.

This was where my husband entered the picture. Although my husband's a painter, photographer, and video editor, I had never considered him in the role of "book cover designer." When he offered to help I was skeptical at first, but then we got into the process and I couldn't help but see that it was a perfect fit. He sat and talked with me about my book, the themes in it, the mood of the story, the motivations and compulsions of the main character, and then he came up with a few ideas that I absolutely loved. After he completed the cover for my second book I vowed never to go back.

This is something some writers might be hesitant about—getting family members (especially a partner), or friends involved with your professional writing life. Sometimes that's valid. I have friends who I already know it would be a bad idea to start a professional relationship with. However, in the case of my husband I knew that I could be honest, blunt even, if I didn't like some element of his design and wanted it changed. If you know that you can be one hundred percent honest with your friend or family member and they won't come away with hurt feelings, and you also know that you're on the same wavelength, then it's a pretty safe bet they would be a good addition to your dream team.

Beta Readers

These are the people I give my book to first, and when I say "first" I mean after I've already gone through a number of rounds of revisions, but before a mass audience sees it. As I've said, every author is different and you have to do what works for you. When it comes to my manuscripts I'm very controlling. I don't let anyone see the rough drafts and I'm very picky about people making suggested changes to me. I work on my manuscripts for a long, long time, and while I could probably be more efficient if I handed over my sloppy first drafts to an editor, I just don't feel comfortable doing things that way. The version I give my beta readers has already usually been revised at least five times.

It goes without saying that my beta readers are people I highly trust. What does need to be mentioned is that they're also fellow writers. Giving your manuscript to friends or family members who aren't writers themselves is good if you just want to get a general impression of how random people might react to the book. But if you truly want to know what's working and what isn't, your beta readers need to be people who write themselves. As an added, almost essential bonus, your fellow writers will understand what a work-in-progress looks like. Most people who are not writers haven't ever seen a book in any other form than the one it comes in all shiny and new straight from the bookstore. Your fellow writers are the ones who have seen the rough stuff before, and will have good suggestions on how to make it better.

You'll notice that my dream team doesn't include a marketing or social media person, or a copy editor. That's because I want to do those things myself. I enjoy those things, and I also don't want them left out of my hands. My dream team reflects my values, and my comfort level. Your dream team should do the same for you.

∾

If you're interested in building your dream team, answer this short list of questions to get the mental process on it started:

Do you have any sort of dream team put together now? If so, list those people by name, role, and function. If not, make a list of the "support people" you feel you do have in place.

What are the aspects of your writing career that you're reasonably sure you will never enjoy or be good at? Who are the people you could delegate those tasks to? For instance, if social media drives you batty, would you be open to the possibility of hiring someone to take that over for you?

What marketing items could be working better for you? How up to date is your website? Do you have vibrant, eye-catching images of your books that you use for promotion? If your answers to those questions are lackluster, would you be open to finding someone who could help in these areas?

If you had all the money and resources in the world at your disposal, who would you hire immediately to help with your marketing? Make a list and be specific about what these people would do for you.

Browse around right now on websites like Fiverr, Creative Market, and Craigslist to see what's out there. Experiment with using the search box and search for things you could use help with, but have never thought of delegating to someone else before.

Part Three
Keeping the Magic Alive

Chapter 20
Experimental Marketing: Trusting the Power of Your Own Curiosity

I t was late summer in San Francisco and foggy. I had a friend staying with me who was visiting from out of town and that August evening we had decided to walk around the Mission to see if we could find anything interesting going on. We happened upon a bookstore that I had walked by many times before, and also heard about from writer friends, but which I had never been in myself. *Let's go in here*, I suggested, and my friend agreed.

The moment we entered I felt it. That impossible-to-describe magnet pull of something drawing me in, further and further, with no obvious reason why. The store was cluttered, stacks of books were everywhere and some of the shelves looked like they were about to fall over. There were a few pieces of grungy furniture thrown here and there with homeless people sleeping on most of them. There was one lone clerk quietly shelving some books up front. My friend and I exchanged looks and moved deeper into the store.

A few minutes later we were interrupted in our browsing by shouting coming from up front. Quickly, we headed that way. An older gentleman, dressed in a natty suit and tie, with a shock of white hair and gold-rimmed spectacles, was leaning over the front counter and shaking the clerk by the lapels of his jacket. "Peter!" he cried. "Did you get the letter? Did you *burn* the letter?"

This man was so agitated. What letter was he talking about? To my growing astonishment, the clerk seemed totally unfazed. The man let go of him and he dusted himself off and smiled. "Yes, of course," he said. "I burned it as soon as I read it." At that, the gentleman with the white hair smiled broadly and then rushed out into the night. My friend and I looked at each other again. *Weird.*

I couldn't help myself. I approached the clerk.

"What was all that about?" I asked him as I deposited the stack of books I wanted to purchase on the counter between us.

"Oh…that. Intrigue and deception." he said indifferently, and began ringing up my books.

The magnet pull of whatever had drawn me into the store was definitely heating up. I looked around as he bagged my books and noticed what I hadn't before. That one of the front windows of the store had a large jagged hole through the middle of it, and shards of glass covered the books on display in that window.

"What happened there?" I asked, pointing to the window.

"Destruction," the clerk answered at once. "And…I guess you could say also…revenge."

"What does that mean?" I was determined to get to the bottom of this.

"There's a woman in the neighborhood who's nursing a vendetta against us. She lost something here…*and* she owns a rival bookstore. So…it makes sense, in a way."

I was beginning to get the feeling that I was talking to a real-life manifestation of the Cheshire Cat.

I also had the definite feeling that this was a place I needed to start frequenting MUCH more often.

When we left I turned to my friend and started gushing. *Wasn't that just the most fabulous place? And what about the clerk? He was fantastic!* I couldn't wait to find out more.

Why would you want to go back there? My friend asked,

confused. *It was filthy. And impossible to find anything. And really, really weird.*

I could easily call this experience the story of my life. Most people cannot understand why I'm interested in the things I am, and why I'm drawn to certain people and places that seem weird or repulsive to them. For a long time, I assumed that I was completely nuts and something was wrong with me, that I had horrible taste. However, once I came into my own as a writer and an artist I realized what was really going on.

I'm a highly creative person.

And all highly creative people are extremely curious.

This personality trait of extreme curiosity is actually a gift, not a liability as I had thought for so long. That weird Wonderland bookstore with the Cheshire Cat I described above? Well, I did end up going back. I went back every week for a year. I made friends with the clerk and he turned out to be a philosopher and a writer, and one of my very great mentors and teachers. He taught me loads about my own intuition. How to tap into it and how to harness it and make it work for me. Every week as I sat with him up at the front desk I scribbled notes about all the wild goings-on in the store, all the crazy characters that I saw come and go and I ended up writing a play using word-for-word dialogue I transcribed from my observations there.

This voracious curiosity is something almost every Highly Sensitive Writer struggles with, and also something almost every Highly Sensitive Writer never realizes is one of their greatest gifts when it comes to marketing work. Most of us tend to think that marketing is a series of formulas, a set of tried-and-true tricks and psychological manipulations that have been proven to sway people to do one thing or another. However, truly great marketing is about experimentation, and it always has a healthy robust sense of curiosity at its core.

That's something a lot of people miss about the marketing genius of Steve Jobs. They tend to concentrate on the fact that he was a perfectionist, and that he demanded total symmetry down to the tiniest details in any product he put out. That was part of his genius, no doubt, but another huge part was his curiosity. He liked to explore new things. When confronted with something new, he liked to poke at it and play with it. He liked to ask questions like, "What if it could do this?" or "Why does it HAVE to be like this, couldn't it be a different way? What would that look like?" By poking and playing and constantly asking questions he uncovered things that most people missed. He saw the Wonderland-type magic in things other people dismissed as weird, or difficult, or just not that interesting.

Truly great marketing is all about using the curiosity every Highly Sensitive Writer is born with to experiment, play, and discover. How do you get started? You use your other big talent as a Highly Sensitive Writer, your intuition.

Remember how I said I immediately felt a magnet pull when I walked in that bookstore? Intuitive people feel that pull (or sometimes a push in the opposite direction) all the time. It's just that we usually ignore it. We've been conditioned by our heavily rational culture not to pay attention to anything that can't be backed up with concrete, tangible evidence that is plainly visible in our material reality. This makes things exceedingly difficult for intuitive people, who live very much through our sixth sense. But if an intuitive, Highly Sensitive Writer can wake up to her own gifts and start putting more trust in herself and her own intuition than she does in what other people are telling her, she'll find that she can feel a pull or push around almost anything, and that these feelings will almost never steer her wrong.

Okay, but how does that tie into marketing a book?

As you get started with book marketing, you will read a ton of stuff about how to do it. There is no shortage of material online or on the bookshelf that can help you. But the thing is, there is a LOT of stuff out there, and almost everyone trumpets their opinions as if their way is the only way and if you do anything else, you're doing it the wrong way.

This is where we come back to intuition and experimentation.

Read everything you can about marketing, yes. But then tap into your intuition. What is your intuition telling you would work best for your book? Put aside everything that everyone says you *should* do. What FEELS right to you? It might be something totally unconventional or something that seems counterintuitive on the surface. Don't let that stop you. Follow your gut and experiment. If your intuition is telling you to start a marketing campaign that has you donating 15% of all sales to endangered animals, then start reaching out to different advocacy groups and see if you get any positive responses. Keep your synchronicity antenna tuned for the slightest vibrations, and make it a point to consciously invite serendipity into your life.

Do this with everything. Follow your curiosity and let your instincts lead you. Constantly ask questions like, "Who would be best served by my book?" "How can I get it into their hands?" Give everything a chance. Do a Goodreads giveaway. Run a Facebook contest. Contact book clubs in your area and see if they're interested in having an author visit their group and give a book talk. You will very likely feel fear come up when trying a lot of these new things out, but don't let that stop you. Feeling nervous anxiety is very different from registering a strong intuitive "no" on something. Whenever you feel that something is a "no" for you, it will come to you calmly and quietly, and you will feel it deep in your gut, just like any other piece of intuitive knowledge that you receive. Nervous anxiety is different. You might get a very strong "yes" leading you down a certain path and still feel nervous and anxious about it. In fact, this is usually the case because whenever we move out of our comfort zone in any way that nervous anxiety kicks in, especially for Highly Sensitive People.

One of my favorite sales gurus of all time, Zig Ziglar, talks about how people in sales can help themselves by shifting perspective. Instead of thinking in terms of failure or success, "this worked" or "that didn't," he says to think of everything as an experiment. When we move into an exploratory state of mind, exactly as if we were scientists in a laboratory tinkering around just to see what happens when we combine X with Y, a lot of the pressure we put on ourselves is relieved and we're free to try new and different things. Instead of "failing" when something doesn't go as planned, we just see it as an experiment that's given us more information about the situation we're examining.

Going back to that weird little bookstore was one of the best decisions I've ever made. Follow your intuition and honor the "pull" you feel to explore certain things. It might be the best thing that's ever happened to your book.

Try these exercises to get your curiosity and intuition moving in high gear. As you write your answers to the questions below let your mind roam free without any limits. This is pure brainstorming, any and all ideas are welcome:

What kind of people would most benefit by reading your book?

Are there any other kinds of people that might benefit too, even if it's not immediately obvious on the surface?

Where do you imagine these people hang out? Are they online somewhere (maybe congregating on a certain forum or in a certain Facebook group) or in a physical space somewhere (maybe at the local farmer's market or the youth rec center in your community)?

How could you start a conversation with these people about your book? Would they be open to receiving a free or discounted copy?

When you think about all the different marketing possibilities are you drawn to anything in particular right away? Are you curious about how a Goodreads giveaway works? Does starting your own Facebook group sound like it might be fun? What imme-

diately pops into your mind and FEELS interesting and a little exciting?

What causes and organizations speak to your heart? Are you drawn to the environment and animals? Have you always wanted to help children? Is there a particular political stance that resonates deeply with you? How could your book help the cause you care the most about? Is there any way you could form a collaborative partnership with an organization around your book that would benefit both of you?

Chapter 21
Slow Marketing: Working with the Energy of Impatience

I t was October 2017 and my newly released addiction memoir, *Between the Shadow and Lo*, had been out for a little over a month. My sales figures were in a slump and I was feeling seriously depressed.

All my writer friends had told me to expect this. *It's quite normal to get that big spike in sales on launch day and then it trickles off after that*, they said. *No one but J.K. Rowling shoots directly onto the bestseller list*, they reassured me. *Being an author is all about being in it for the long term*, they added. *You gain readers—and traction—slowly over time.*

I got it. I totally understood what they were saying.

But I still felt like crap.

Between the Shadow and Lo was not my first book, and so this was not my first dance with fluctuating Kindle sales. My first book had come out a year earlier, in 2016. *The INFJ Writer* started off slowly and did gain traction over time, just as my writer friends told me would happen. But, the thing was, I didn't have as much emotional involvement with that book. I wasn't worried what people would think of me after they read it.

My addiction memoir was a different story.

So, it was easy for me to go from "rational" and "detached" into "panicky" and "despairing" very quickly. Similarly, it was very hard for my brain to separate the impersonal data of my sales figures from the emotional way that I felt about the book. As so often happens when we're already self-conscious from the first moment that we enter a situation, I was ready to draw conclusions about proof of the book's flaws from that impersonal data.

But then, I discovered new information, and that new information helped me to see the real problem, the real reason I had gone so wrong in the first place.

I was madly hunting around on the internet for anything I could do to improve my Kindle sales rankings and I stumbled across a few great posts from Dave over at Kindlepreneur. Now, in the past, I had visited Dave's site and I ALWAYS came away with helpful information, but it was also information that I needed time to absorb and digest properly. Dave's methods are heavily infused with practical nuts-and-bolts research and strategies that he's implemented in real time to gauge results. "Practical," "nuts-and-bolts," and "real time" are all concepts that I've struggled with my whole life. I do much better with "abstract," "big picture," and "emotion." So, it wasn't surprising that I had probably seen these posts from Dave before, but failed to truly understand the valuable information he was giving me.

Dave said that one of the most effective factors of success when it came to Kindle rankings were the keywords you used and the categories you chose for the book. This was not entirely new information to me. I had worked for startups for years and, in fact, had worked on many SEO (search engine optimization) projects at my current day job. I knew a lot about the power of keywords. I also knew very well that keywords were one of the main reasons my first book had done (and was doing) so well. A lot of people online were searching for "INFJ" paired with the word "writer." My title alone on that book was bringing in new readers.

So why had I completely neglected this facet of things as I was preparing to push the "publish" button on my memoir?

Because I was way more emotional about everything.

Between the Shadow and Lo was a book I had worked on for a long time. It was a book that had pushed me through countless stages of fear and self-doubt. I was worried what my family would think, what my friends would think, even what people from my small hometown would think. That book revealed every nitty gritty detail of all the crazy (and sometimes horrible) things I had done as an alcoholic. It contained explicitly sexual subject matter, as well as material about crime and drug abuse. I was proud of it and I wanted to release it into the world, but I was also terrified of what the world would think, and say, after reading it.

So, that morning when I launched my book, as I was preparing to hit the "publish" button, I wasn't thinking clearly. I didn't realize it at the time, but I was almost purely in survival mode. I was consumed with waves of elation and giddiness, and then felt like a bucket of ice water had been dumped on me as the waves bloomed and crashed over my head, leaving me in a state of fear and trepidation. My hands were shaking, my mouth was dry, and I felt slightly nauseous that entire day.

A month later I couldn't recall at all what keywords I had chosen, or even in what categories I had placed the book.

When I went back and checked I was shocked.

Here were my keywords:

- *Seattle*
- *Alcoholism*
- *Alcoholic*
- *Depression*
- *Fiction*
- *Novel*
- *Women's issues*

My categories were:

- *Fiction – Contemporary*
- *Fiction – Women's Fiction*

I probably couldn't have picked worse keywords and categories if I had tried.

What wasn't so surprising was that now—even though I knew I needed to come up with something much better—I didn't have that great of an idea of where to start. I had been so consumed not only with the emotional tornado I was going through about publishing the book, but also dealing with the last-minute big items (final touches on formatting and cover design, trying to get the e-book description to sync up with the paperback description on Amazon, writing the release announcements for my blog and social media), that keywords and categories had been the last thing on my mind.

So, when I was confronted with those choices during the publishing process I had obviously just grabbed the first words I could think of and never looked back.

Until now, a month later, when I was studying the blunders I had made in this area in the rear-view mirror.

This was when I learned a hugely important lesson about slowing down during the marketing process. If I had slowed down enough before I hit "publish" I would have decided on better keywords and categories right from the start. If I had taken a step back, and taken a few deep breaths, I would have allowed myself to take the time I needed to properly research what keywords and categories would best apply to my book.

That said, instead of beating myself up with judgment in this moment and wasting even more time, I knew the best thing would be to slow down and forgive myself for making a mistake, and then give myself the time I needed to correct it.

I spent a week researching keywords, reading even more of Dave's Kindlepreneur posts, and looking around at dozens of other memoirs and autobiographical novels that were similar to mine to see what those authors were doing. Ultimately, it was the best use of my time and my book benefited from it, *significantly*.

After my week of research, I had confirmation that women's fiction and contemporary fiction really were probably the two worst categories I could have picked. The competition in both was overwhelming and fierce. My book ranked somewhere around #33,000 in the list of available titles. Plus, my memoir didn't even really fit into either of those genres, so the readers who were browsing through them wouldn't have been that interested anyway even if they had—by some miracle—stumbled across my book.

With my new knowledge of categories and how they worked, I now placed my book into:

- *Health – Addiction and Recovery – Alcoholism*
- *Health – Psychology – Mental Health – Mental Illness*

These are two categories that much more aptly express what the book deals with and what the book is actually about.

After making the switch, my book now ranked as #152 and #621 in each category, respectively. I still wasn't a #1 bestseller, but my book stood a MUCH greater chance of being discovered than if I had been ranked somewhere around #33,000.

Then, I changed my keywords to:

- *Addiction memoirs*
- *Dark humor*
- *Urban life*
- *Transgressive fiction*
- *Alcoholism*
- *Substance abuse*
- *Addiction recovery*

Acting on Dave's Kindlepreneur advice, I also listed three

well-known transgressive fiction authors in my Amazon book description who had written similar books to mine, so that readers would know "what kind of book" they were in for if they gave my memoir a chance.

Now, when I checked the Amazon Kindle store, my book came up on the first page for "transgressive fiction" results, right alongside Charles Bukowski, one of the authors I had listed on my description page.

These small, but essential, changes in my keywords and categories changed the game for me. I went from selling zero books at all to selling one or two books every few days. Again, I realize these are not James Patterson-like sales figures, but I'm not going for superstar author status. I just want to cultivate an audience, any audience. To me, seeing an increase of selling one to two books every few days over zero, just from making a few tweaks to my keywords and categories, was a momentous marketing moment.

Writers don't need to memorize all the latest keyword marketing hacks available. The online world is a constantly changing entity. Its very nature is to grow and evolve and shed old methods and strategies almost as fast as people can discover them. The books and articles you'll read about mastering the latest trending marketing hacks will all be outdated in just a couple of years. Instead, your writing career will be much better served by remembering:

The best thing you can do in marketing work is to slow down and keep your center strong.

The next best thing you can do is realize that marketing work is always fluid, and nothing is set in stone. If you make a mistake or recognize that you could be doing something better, you can always refocus your attention on the issue and improve it.

Too much of the time, we jump the gun with our marketing efforts because they make us feel uncomfortable or inadequate in some way and so we try to rush through them. And then we're embarrassed by how much we don't know, so we never go back to correct our mistakes. But it doesn't have to be this way. If you slow down and center your energy by checking in with yourself and breathing deeply, your focus and attention will be strong instead of scattered. Your personal will has a better chance of following your true intentions instead of dissipating into panic and fear.

Use these quick exercises to see where you fall on the "strong" versus "scattered" spectrum:

If you're in the process of querying your book, or trying to market your book, do you feel like you have a clear idea of what genre you story falls into? On a scale of 1 to 10, how clear are you on that?

Do you have a clear idea of who your ideal reader might be? Are there other types of readers out there who you might not have thought of because you're too busy focusing on the ideal?

Are there any "marketing tasks" that you currently rush through because you dislike them? Do you ignore other facets of marketing altogether because they make you uncomfortable? Can you make a list of those things that only receive the impatient end of your energy?

Is there any area of your marketing that you actually would like to learn more about, but you've been putting off because you don't have the time? Can you commit to moving something else off of your plate for a week or two in order to make the time you need to do it?

Chapter 22
Detached Marketing: How to Stop Banging Your Head Against Doors that Don't Want to Open

In July of 2015 I was floundering. I had just given birth to my son five months before and I had been back at my day job for about six weeks after a long maternity leave. My son was one of those babies that doesn't sleep, ever. Five months in and he was still waking up five or six times (or more) at night, every night. I was getting up with him, working the 9-5, and also trying to pick back up with my coaching work on the side.

I was exhausted.

I was so tired on such a constant basis that sleep deprivation had become a way of life. Cars routinely honked at me in traffic when I sat still at green lights. I couldn't remember things people had told me half an hour ago. I could fall asleep anywhere—sitting up, in a meeting, at my desk. I felt like the dead guy in *Weekend at Bernie's* who gets carted around everywhere.

Along with the other parts of my life that needed attention was the querying process. I had finished four novels in the past nine years and had been actively querying on three of them for the past five. My first novel in particular was the book I really wanted to get out there. *Between the Shadow and Lo* is the book I've already mentioned numerous times. It was the story that was the hardest for me to tell, and the most emotionally charged. The novel was really a memoir in disguise, all about the intense years I had spent in my early 20s as an alcoholic in Seattle. It was the book I wrote in my first writing program, and the book that had cracked my heart wide open and forced me to open a vein onto the page.

I was fiercely proud of that book, and also terrified of the reactions people might have to it. I desperately wanted to see it in print before I died, and also stricken at the thought that members of my family might actually read it. It was dark, gritty, and extremely graphic in places. It was a story in which I unleashed my shadow side, in a way I never had before.

To say that book was carrying a bit of my emotional baggage was the understatement of the century.

I had been querying on the book for about five years at that point. When I read blog posts by writers that said they had received 75 (omg! 75!) rejections before their novel was accepted I half laughed and half imagined myself strangling them. I had received over 200 rejections, and not even one person asked to see a partial. I had queried *everybody* even remotely in the range of my subject matter. My book fell squarely into the genre of "transgressive fiction" but I had only located five or six agents who were looking for that type of thing. Desperate to get a bite from anyone, I stretched the limits of my query and described my book as "dark fiction," "serious women's fiction," and even "urban fantasy" at one point (hoping some of the weirder elements might come across as fantastical), all to no avail. No one was interested. No one.

So, I was sleep deprived, low on money as usual, struggling to breastfeed a baby while holding down a day job and a side business, and no one in the entire world wanted to read my novel.

I was in a bad place.

But, unbeknownst to me at the time, this "bad place" was actually the best place I could have been in. What I didn't realize at the time was that my old patterns had ceased working. I had been banging my head against the door of the publishing world, begging for it to open, for someone to please let me in, and never seeing that there was a reason that door was remaining closed to me.

During this time too, I started listening to webinars and podcasts in the late afternoon while I was finishing up routine paperwork tasks at my desk. I had started out listening to people who were successful coaches offering business-building advice and this had taken me down all kinds of different avenues. One day I ended up listening to a webinar on how to bring in more clients. The woman who was giving advice said, "You need to put a product out there. It doesn't have to be perfect. As long as it's useful, it can be simple and to the point. Just get something out there!"

It might have been because I was so sleep deprived, but something about her statement got through my normal resistance to all sales and marketing information. I kept hearing her words echo in my head. "It doesn't have to be perfect...as long as it's useful...It doesn't have to be perfect...as long as it's useful..."

When I thought about the gritty dark novel that held all of my emotional baggage, and that no one apparently wanted, I felt heavy, depressed, and hopeless. When I thought about making a new thing—writing a new book—that didn't have to be perfect and could just be a useful product that was meant to help somebody, I felt way different. I felt lighter, excited, and hopeful.

It felt like, while I was sitting on the floor sobbing pathetically because no one would open the publishing world door to me, another door had opened quietly behind me and now sunlight was streaming in. When I turned around, I saw a friendly hand waving me through. "Come on in here..." the hand said. "There's different stuff in here that you might have some fun with." It felt like I was a kid again, and maybe, just possibly, there was something magical within my reach.

That was how I started writing my book, *The INFJ Writer*, which was the fifth book I ever wrote, but the first book I ever published. I wrote the book in six weeks at a breakneck pace, but I didn't feel any resistance to it at all. I was still totally sleep deprived, which I think actually helped because I was too tired to worry about perfectionism. But what really did the trick was my mindset. I never thought of *The INFJ Writer* as my masterpiece, or my life's work. I never considered it my "debut novel" or even my first book. All of those heavy expectations had been sunk into the dark, gritty novel about my alcoholic life in Seattle. *The INFJ Writer*, instead, was just what that woman said it could be in the webinar that changed my perspective. It was a simple, useful product that I knew could help people. No more and no less.

Well, months after I self-published *The INFJ Writer*, I realized that it wasn't just a product. I had gotten too many heartfelt emails from people who told me it had seriously helped them change their writing life for the better. I saw then that *The INFJ Writer* was a work of art, and it was a work that came directly from my heart and soul. The only difference between *The INFJ Writer* and my dark, gritty novel was that I hadn't placed two tons of expectations and fears on the book before it even had a chance to find any readers.

This is the power of detachment at work.

If you've ever studied Buddhism, even casually, you know that detachment is a big thing for the Buddhists. We're all trapped in this cycle of constant pain and suffering that we call life because we get attached to things in our own minds. We decide that things have to be a certain way before we're happy or that we have to have certain things before we can feel secure. Once this is explained to you, you get it on a deep level. Every person who is human has gone through this, so it's easily recognizable. *A-ha!* you think. *That's what's been going on all along. I'm too attached. Ok, cool. I'll just detach like those peaceful Zen meditation folks I see online and in yoga class and my life will become radically better.*

Easier said than done.

In the case of me and my dark, gritty novel, I couldn't just magically detach from it. As I've mentioned in previous chapters, I put *Between the Shadow and Lo* out in 2017 and I still had a lot of my old hang-ups about it. To get around all the baggage of that book, I had to make something totally new. I had to create a book that was completely fresh and put it out there with as little expectation as possible. *The INFJ Writer* felt like a "practice" book to me, an experiment just to see if I could put something out there that would help people. What I didn't anticipate was that my little experiment would give me the confidence to move forward with the dark, gritty novel that I had been stalled out on for so long.

My practice of detachment was strengthened even more when I read *The Hustle Economy* by Jason Oberholtzer and I started making more of the shift from writer to writer-as-entrepreneur. Made up of various essays from writers, artists, and other creators, *The Hustle Economy* urges us to keep making things and pushing our creations out into the world. Instead of adhering to the old model, which says that writers should strive to put out a perfect masterpiece that stands the test of the ages and remains timeless and iconic hundreds of years later, the new model says that millions of new things are being created and consumed on the internet every day. Your work doesn't have to be perfect, it just has to be pretty damn good.

As a perfectionist, you know the difference between "perfect" and "pretty damn good" might as well be as wide as the Atlantic Ocean. And let me tell you, striving to hit "pretty damn good" takes a huge amount of pressure off.

The way to get started on this is to step away from whatever "masterpiece" you've been sweating over up until this point. You know what I'm talking about—the book that is actually totally finished but that you keep messing with anyway because you're not getting any bites on it from agents, or you're filled with self-doubt about what your family might think if they read it. Leave that project alone for a while and start imagining something new. Start thinking about something fresh and creative you could write that you might not be so attached to. Maybe it's a short e-book, or a blog you could start anonymously. Maybe it's a short story that you could use as a way of experimenting with submitting to online magazines or literary journals. Whatever it is, it should be something that you care about, but you're not willing to die over. Something that, if it gets rejected, you'll still be okay.

Stepping back, working on something new, and bringing the imagination and playfulness back into your writing can go a long way toward dissolving that heavy personal investment in your work that might be causing you problems.

~

Play around with these exercises and see what ideas come up for you:

Is there a specific book you're trying to push out into the world that is giving you a major headache? What would it feel like to step away from that book and not look at it at all for two months?

Get a piece of blank paper and write this statement five times:

"Once my book is published I want it to..."

Then go back and fill in the blanks with all the things you want your book to do. Keep writing that statement and filling in the blanks until you run out of things you want your book to do. Now read back over what you wrote. Are there any expectations in there that seem unrealistic? Are there any expectations in there that actually aren't yours, and might be coming from your parents or your peer group?

Now write this statement:

"The way you can tell that a book is successful is if it..."

Repeat the exercise above by filling in the blanks with all the statements that describe what you think a successful book looks like.

Now read over those statements. Are all of those statements really true? How do you know they're true? How did you come to decide that's what a successful book should look like?

Firefly Magic

Now make a list of numbers, one through ten. Write the first ten things that occur to you that you could create or build or put together that might impact someone else positively, and that you could put out into the world within one to two months. Read back over your list. What draws you the most strongly? Is there anything that surprises you? Pick one thing that you would seriously consider getting started on.

Chapter 23
Purposeful Marketing: Finding Your USP

From the time I was a teenager up until my mid-30s, I felt like I had two things severely wrong with me. One: I was weird. Not in a cute, quirky way like the adorable sidekick in a teen movie, but in a very bad "uncool" way. I was awkward in my social interactions and I was interested in things that it seemed no one else was. I was also *not* interested in the things everyone else *was* interested in—sports, celebrities, fashion, etc. This weird streak in me never went away. I didn't grow out of it. I just learned to hide it better, almost supernaturally better, and blend in like a chameleon wherever I happened to be.

The second thing that was wrong revolved around writing. I wanted to write more than anything else in life. I wanted it with my entire heart and soul. However, I couldn't write. I would write a paragraph or two and immediately give up. It was bad. I knew it was bad. And when I showed it to other people I could tell that, even if maybe it wasn't as bad as I thought, it still wasn't very good.

So, those were my two things. My two huge glaring defects. I was a total weirdo, AND a failed writer.

For years, I hid these things from people. I was so ashamed. I just couldn't talk about it, not even to my closest friends. And I lived in terror of anyone else ever finding out.

Then, in 2006, at the age of 27, I finally started writing. I joined a writing program where we showed up to write for one hour together once a week and it actually seemed to work. I was still a horrible writer (in my mind) but at least I *was* writing. It was progress.

But the weirdo thing didn't go away and, unlike the writing, it wasn't getting any better. In fact, I was feeling even more down about it because I had kind of expected that I might meet more weird people in my writing program. And while, yes, there were some offbeat people there, I still felt out of place. There was still something that I just couldn't put my finger on, some way in which I was different that was just so hard to deal with.

Then, in 2010, I started spending a lot of time on the internet. I started reading all sorts of blogs and prying into narrow niche corners of the online world, learning about personality, psychology, and what made people tick. I had heard of Myers-Briggs before, it wasn't a new thing, but in 2010 and then into 2011 it seemed like more information was popping up about it online. When I took the test, got the result "INFJ," and then started researching what that meant in earnest, everything changed for me.

Yes, I was different. No, it was not my imagination.

Even better, there were others out there. I wasn't alone.

This had such a huge impact on me that I started devouring anything INFJ-related I could find. Unfortunately, there were hardly any books about INFJs listed on Amazon. This was doubly sad for me because I was a hardcore bookworm and had been since the age of six. Reading books was how I learned about things. It was another quirky aspect of my nerdy nature that served me extremely well in school, but which I was still trying to figure out how to use in real life. I'd had four retail jobs and four office jobs at this point, and not one of my co-workers or managers at those jobs had seemed to care one bit that I could chew my way through entire dry dusty volumes of information with no problem. And one of those jobs was at a bookstore. I figured if the bookstore didn't care about my freakish reading skill, then I was definitely out of luck when it came to this being a marketable trait.

So, when I could only find a handful of books on Myers-Briggs on Amazon at that time, and all of them seemed to be vague and general and not really concentrated on INFJs in particular, I was deeply disappointed.

All in all, I had three big problems:

1. I felt like a weirdo freak.
2. I had huge issues with writer's block and I wasn't sure why.
3. I was bummed that I couldn't find a really good book on INFJs and other intuitive personalities.

Two personal defects and one big feeling of lack.

It might sound odd, but these three problems are what helped me find my Unique Spiritual Purpose.

What is a Unique Spiritual Purpose? Let's back up for a moment. In the marketing world, USP stands for *Unique Selling Proposition*. A Unique Selling Proposition is the trait (or collection of traits) that makes a product different, better, and more special than its competitors. It's the secret sauce. Anyone going into business selling anything quickly learns that figuring out a product's Unique Selling Proposition is essential to coming up with a marketing plan that will actually work.

For Highly Sensitive Writers, the term Unique Selling Proposition tends to make our eyes glaze over. We could not care less about what the whizzbang doohickey on the latest tech gadget does or how much it costs. To us, it all sounds like figuring out how to sell things to people who probably don't really need those things.

But a Unique Spiritual Purpose is different. It's in the same ballpark as Unique Selling Proposition, but it's fundamentally about something much larger and more meaningful. A Unique Spiritual Purpose is the message that only you can deliver to people who are in need of it. A Unique Spiritual Purpose always helps people first, and focuses on expanding itself second. A Unique Spiritual Purpose works in service and brings light and hope and healing to those it serves.

Every single Highly Sensitive Writer has a Unique Spiritual Purpose.

Finding your Unique Spiritual Purpose as a Highly Sensitive Writer will benefit you just as much as a Unique Selling Proposition benefits a business person ready to go out and sell their product. Once you know and fully understand the Unique Spiritual Purpose of your work, you will know who needs it the most. You will start to get ideas on how to find those people. You will gain confidence and show up in the places those people hang out. You will feel good about putting your work out there, telling people you have a book and they should buy it, and seeing how each piece of your writing work fits into the whole of your writer path.

But, how do you figure out your Unique Spiritual Purpose?

You look honestly at your own darkness, and your own disappointments.

For me, my Unique Spiritual Purpose started making itself evident to me a year or two after I first looked on Amazon and couldn't find the book I wanted on INFJs. I was still feeling like a weirdo, and still struggling with writer's block from time to time. I had started a blog and then a fledgling business coaching other writers. The writers who came to me as clients had eerily similar problems. They all felt like weirdoes too. They all suffered from writer's block. When I found out that they were also all intuitive personality types, the light went on for me.

And then, as I mentioned in a previous chapter, I realized I possibly had something I could make into a book that would be useful to people, even if it wasn't perfect.

What if I wrote a book about being an INFJ and struggling

with writer's block? I thought to myself. *What if I included my own stories in that book of feeling like a weirdo and someone who would never belong? What if I named and honestly talked about all of the embarrassment, shame, fear, and resistance I had experienced because of these things?*

That was the book I had so desperately searched for and wanted to find right after I found out I was an INFJ. And if I wasn't alone in the extremely weird personality quirks that came along with being an INFJ, then chances were high that I wasn't alone in the rest of it either.

That was how my book, *The INFJ Writer*, was born.

I didn't have a marketing plan. I didn't have a marketing budget. In fact, I didn't know the first thing about marketing. When I went online and looked up book marketing, it made me feel slightly nauseous and definitely unenthused. I didn't want to aggressively push my book onto people who didn't want it. I didn't want to compete in the confusing numbers game of how to become a bestseller on Amazon in 24 hours. That energy of seeking dominance, trying to win the game, and earning status points didn't appeal to me at all.

But, I did want the INFJ writers out there to find and read my book. Because I knew in my heart and my gut that it could help them.

So instead of a Unique Selling Proposition—instead of figuring out ways to compete with all the other books out there in the introvert, Highly Sensitive Person, Myers-Briggs space—I focused instead on my Unique Spiritual Purpose. This is what I wrote down as my mission:

To find and help all the other INFJ (and INFP) writers out there who feel misunderstood, alone, and confused. To show these people strategies and practices that will actually help them begin to write again. To reassure them that they are beautiful, they belong, and they each have artistic gifts that the world badly needs.

Firefly Magic

This was my Unique Spiritual Purpose behind *The INFJ Writer*, and it still is. Once I put these statements into play, everything became very clear. Competition was a complete non-issue. No one could compete with me, because each person on earth has their own Unique Spiritual Purpose. The only reason I had a leg up was because I had actually articulated mine.

As a Highly Sensitive Writer, you have a Unique Spiritual Purpose. Every one of the books you write will also have a Unique Spiritual Purpose. And every one might be different. Your first book might be a nonfiction collection of essays with the Unique Spiritual Purpose of helping to heal women suffering from eating disorders. Your second book might be a romantic comedy meant to help people tap into the healing power of laughter, while also giving them hope that a loving partner can be found and good relationships do exist. A Highly Sensitive Writer's Unique Spiritual Purpose is fluid and creative. It crosses genres and pushes boundaries. You will not be able to find your Unique Spiritual Purpose by copying something that someone else is doing.

Your Unique Spiritual Purpose is yours, and yours alone.

Here are some exercises to get you started on finding, and articulating, your Unique Spiritual Purpose:

Write down two or three big problems you have always struggled with—whether personal problems like body image issues or societal problems like racism and sexism. Then make a list of people you have met or read about who are struggling with the very same problems.

Take 20 minutes when you are alone and in a calm space to journal about your own personal shame. Be as honest as you possibly can on the page, don't hold anything back. If you feel wrong or broken somehow, talk about how wrong or broken you feel. On the other hand, if you feel that you were in the right about something and you were the one wronged, talk about that. When you're done writing, take another 10 minutes and sit quietly or go for a walk by yourself and consider all the other people in the world who might be feeling a similar kind of shame.

If you've already written a book, or you're working on one now, start thinking about the deeper themes of that book. What do you want people to do when they read it: Laugh? Learn? Shift perspective on a certain issue? Why does it mean so much to you that people do this particular thing? How will they be helped by doing this particular thing? When you have a little bit of an idea coming clear about it, sit down and journal about your thoughts.

Try writing out your own Unique Spiritual Purpose for yourself as a writer, or for the book you're working on at the moment or currently trying to sell.

Chapter 24
Sacred Selling: Marketing as a Part of Your Spiritual Practice

It was the early spring of 2013 and I was sequestered away from the world at a beach house in Stinson Beach, California, a tiny coastal community about 20 miles north of San Francisco. To get to Stinson Beach, I had driven over the Golden Gate Bridge and then up into the hills, finally snaking along the coast, hugging the side of land that dropped down to the ocean on my left. The beach house was right outside of the small village that made up Stinson Beach, one side of the house facing the sea and the other side protected by a tall fence and trees. There was no TV or radio in the house, and no internet. Just a fireplace, a fridge stocked with food, and a wall of bookshelves.

It felt like heaven.

Every year, one of my best friends celebrated her birthday by renting one of these extremely private little beach houses at Stinson. She invited her closest friends (all of who loved to cook) and we settled in for a long weekend of delicious food, board games, coloring, jacuzzi-soaking, and frequent walks on the beach. I had been looking forward even more than usual to this year's Stinson getaway because I was feeling burnt out. On everything. Work at my day job had been hectic, my volunteer activities had mushroomed out of control, and I never seemed to be able to find enough time for my writing. I was tired and stressed and just over it. I badly needed to recharge.

But…I didn't want to *just* recharge. Part of me didn't want to go back out into the world, period. It was tough out there. So many people were so difficult to deal with. I had a busy life filled with endless demands, and most of those demands came from other people. On a daily basis I dealt with frustration, anger, fear, resignation, cynicism, and disappointment, some of it coming from me and some of it from others. Why couldn't I just stay somewhere like the Stinson beach house forever? Why couldn't I adopt the life of a monk or a hermit and live up on an isolated mountaintop, or perhaps in a cave? I would need only the bare necessities and I would fill my days with the things I really cared about: contemplation, and writing.

It was in this mood that I got up from the coloring table and began to browse the bookshelves my first morning at Stinson. One book immediately caught my eye. It was *A Path with Heart* by Jack Kornfield. I had seen Jack Kornfield speak at one of his regular Monday night lectures at Spirit Rock just a couple of years before and been impressed. The things he said resonated with me and I liked his energy. I felt like I could trust him. So, frustrated with my life and looking for answers, I picked *A Path with Heart* off the shelf.

Jack Kornfield gave me the mental sustenance I badly needed in that moment, but he also gave me much more. I had gone into the book thinking that my problem was with the world, and all the people in it. *Humans were too unpredictable*, I had thought, *and too annoying to deal with every day*. The whole swirl of emotions that dipped toward the negative were too much for me. The constant turmoil of the human drama encroached on my time, and drained my emotional resources. Everything would be solved if I could just withdraw from the world and be a one-woman island.

Reading *A Path with Heart* changed my perspective. Kornfield explained that it's not necessary to live in a monastery or take extreme vows of poverty or chastity in order to commit to a spiritual life. In fact, he said, most people not only can't do this, they shouldn't. We're not meant to be a planet made up of one hundred percent hermits. The very opposite is true. We are meant to be in relationship with each, with all of the turmoil and drama—and joy —that brings. We are meant to discuss and debate, and negotiate and misunderstand each other, and come back to clarity, over and over again. This is how we learn and grow. This is how we evolve.

The exact phrase Kornfield used was "going out into the marketplace" and by that he meant going out and getting involved in the business of life. That phrase stayed with me, and echoed a few different themes that were unique to my own process of growth. For many years I had struggled with limiting beliefs about business and money, assuming that both were "unspiritual" and solely the province of those who were greedy, status-hungry, and insensitive to the feelings of others. In the next few years I continued to work on my belief systems and choose new viewpoints, but I always came back to Jack Kornfield's phrase of "going out into the marketplace." Could it be that conducting business could also be part of one's spiritual practice? Something in me said, yes, it definitely could.

This was how I first saw that topics I thought I'd never have any interest in (selling and marketing) could be an integral part of something deep within that fed my soul (my relationship to spirit). Then, in 2016, when I started publishing my books, I knew I needed to learn more about how selling and marketing could be combined with spirit.

In my writing work, I had no problem finding spirit. I wrote to help people, in one way or another, and so that part felt easy. But the marketing of my book—the work I needed to do to *sell* the book—there I was stumbling. My old limiting beliefs were kicking in. Salespeople were only out for themselves, and business was a cold, impersonal process made up of people looking for weaknesses to exploit. I felt stressed and threatened by the whole thing. I fell back on my tried-and-true defense mechanism. I wanted to withdraw completely.

So, using my imagination, I took myself back to that Stinson beach house where I had been three years earlier. I imagined what my life would have been like if I had never left the Stinson beach house. I could have had all my food delivered and only had the most basic of interaction with other humans. I would have written, but I wouldn't have published anything. I wouldn't have worked on my blog, or interacted on social media, or tried to tell anyone about any of my ideas. Everything would have been way easier. However, I could also see that my potential of helping anyone would have been drastically reduced. If I'd had an awesome idea for an exercise that a Highly Sensitive Writer could use to tap into their own potential, that idea would have stayed closeted in my notebook, and finally died with me, after my long life as a hermit at the beach house ended and some strangers came to clean everything out.

Jack Kornfield's advice had been right for me then, and it was right for me now. The life of a hermit wasn't for me. As a writer, my calling was to write things and then *go out into the marketplace and sell them*.

This is part of the calling of every writer.

It doesn't matter what you write—romance novels, creative nonfiction, poetry, or cookbooks—if you are writing then you are writing *to be read*. The missing puzzle piece you need to complete your natural cycle as a creative being is the reader. And finding readers is part of the process. Exploring the world, making connections, reaching out to people, *marketing your book* is what finding readers is all about. In an energetic sense, it is you showing up at the market, picking your stall, setting up your table, putting the things you have created on that table, and then smiling and chatting with the people who pass by, actively looking for that connection with someone who shows interest.

Every part of this process is tied to your relationship with spirit. Hiring an editor and a cover designer to make your book the best it can be is nurturing a healthy pride in your work. Thinking up catchy tag lines and blurbs for your book is engaging your creative faculties and pushing them to stretch and grow. Doing a book launch and creating different types of thoughtful marketing campaigns is opening yourself up to the world and getting comfortable with vulnerability. Building a following on social media (tweeting at people, liking posts, commenting, sharing) is making yourself available for connection and friendship.

Every time you immerse yourself in marketing work with integrity, an open heart, and the desire to be of service to yourself and others, you are growing and evolving as a human being.

Staying stuck in unhelpful beliefs about how marketing is "bad" or you "hate it" is the energetic equivalent of either kicking and screaming on the floor, or sitting up in your room sulking.

That's exactly what I was doing when I told myself I wanted to withdraw from the world forever on that long-ago weekend at Stinson Beach. It's also what I was doing when I published my first book and then conveniently didn't tell anyone about it.

So, I decided to get busy. I packed up my things and walked to the marketplace. I worked on my stall (my blog) and then I started setting out my wares (my articles and my book on Amazon). I chatted with the people who passed by (through blog comments, or Facebook and Twitter) and concentrated on bringing as much clarity as I could to what I was selling (through website design and marketing blurbs about my book and my services). I did this over and over again. I did it when I wasn't feeling it and when I was busy with life and stressed. And as much as I could, with every one of these things, I came back to my relationship with spirit and centered myself in the energy of service.

I don't feel like marketing is "bad" now. In fact, I get excited about learning new things about selling and marketing all the time. I don't see business people as "separate" from me anymore either, or like I couldn't possibly have anything to talk about with them. I see myself as one of them. Being a business person doesn't change my character or the essence of who I am. It's just another role I play, like being a wife, a mother, a friend, or a mentor. It doesn't define me. It's a tool I use to do my work here to the best of my ability.

Marketing and selling are skills. They are tools available to you to enhance your writer's toolbox. That's all. You can feel threatened by them and decide you don't like them and ignore them as much as you can, probably forever. Or you can get curious. You can pick them up and try them out. You can see what they feel like in your hands and get excited about all the cool things you can do with them.

How you feel about marketing and selling your work is a choice. And no one else is going to make it for you. The choice is yours and the time is now. So…are you going to hold yourself back from the world? Or will you join me in the marketplace?

I'll be there with my stall open, as always, ready to sell. I hope I see you there.

More Books on Writing, Creativity, and Intuition
By Lauren Sapala

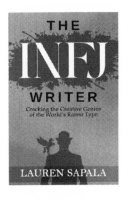

The INFJ Writer – INFJ writers don't think like anyone else, and their highly creative brains take a toll on them that they rarely share with the outside world. Any writer with the self-awareness to identify as highly sensitive and intuitive will benefit from this book that helps them to find their own magic, and to finally use it to build the creative life that actually works for them.

The INFJ Revolution – Although ever-growing numbers of INFJs are waking up to the power of our intuitive gifts, we continue to struggle in a culture that does not value intuition. Only by moving beyond limiting mindsets and beliefs can INFJs fulfill their purpose as the healers of the world, reclaim their power, and step into the role of the leaders they were always meant to be.

Available on Amazon in ebook and paperback.

Bibliography

Anderson, Chris. *The Long Tail: Why the Future of Business Is Selling Less of More*. Hachette Books, 2008

Baron, Eric. *Selling Is a Team Sport: Turn Your Whole Organization into a Living, Breathing Selling Machine*. Crown Business, 2000

Bettger, Frank. *How I Raised Myself from Failure to Success in Selling*. Prentice Hall, 1975

Blount, Jeb. *Fanatical Prospecting: The Ultimate Guide to Opening Sales Conversations and Filling the Pipeline by Leveraging Social Selling, Telephone, Email, Text, and Cold Calling*. Wiley, 2015

Bonanno, Joseph. *A Man of Honor: The Autobiography of Joseph Bonanno*. St. Martin's Press, 2003

Bosworth, Michael T. *CustomerCentric Selling*. McGraw-Hill, 2010

Broughton, Philip Delves. *The Art of the Sale: Learning from the Masters about the Business of Life*. Penguin Books, 2013

Davila, Randy. *Think Like a Publisher: 33 Essential Tips to Write, Promote & Sell Your Book*. Hierophant Publishing, 2013

Eisler, Barry and Konrath, Joe. *Be the Monkey: A Conversation about the New World of Publishing*. Amazon Digital Services, LLC, 2011

Florida, Richard. *The Rise of the Creative Class—Revisited: Revised and Expanded*. Basic Books, 2014

Gitomer, Jeffrey. *Little Red Book of Sales Answers: 99.5 Real Life Answers that Make Sense, Make Sales, and Make Money*. FT Press, 2006

Guo, Charlie. *Unscalable*. Inkshares, 2016

Kawasaki, Guy (and Welch, Shawn). *APE: Author, Publisher, Entrepreneur: How to Publish a Book*. Nononina Press, 2012

Kennedy, Dan. S. *The Ultimate Marketing Plan: Target Your Audience! Get Out Your Message! Build Your Brand!* Adams Media, 2011

Klaff, Oren. *Pitch Anything: An Innovative Method for Presenting, Persuading, and Winning the Deal*. McGraw-Hill, 2011

Konrath, J.A. *The Newbie's Guide to Publishing*. Amazon Digital Services, LLC, 2010

Kornfield, Jack. *A Path with Heart: A Guide through the Perils and Promises of Spiritual Life*. Bantam, 1993

Myss, Caroline. *Anatomy of the Spirit: The Seven Stages of Power and Healing*. Harmony, 1996

Bibliography

Pine, B. Joseph (and Gilmore, James H.) *The Experience Economy: Work Is Theatre & Every Business a Stage*. Harvard Business School Press, 1999

Oberholtzer, Jason. *The Hustle Economy: Transforming Your Creativity into a Career*. Running Press, 2016

Pink, Daniel H. *To Sell Is Human: The Surprising Truth about Moving Others*. Riverhead Books, 2013

Rackham, Neil. *SPIN Selling: Situation Problem Implication Need-payoff*. McGraw-Hill, 1988

Richardson, Linda. *Sales Coaching: Making the Great Leap from Sales Manager to Sales Coach*. McGraw-Hill, 2008

Scott, David Meerman. *The New Rules of Marketing and PR: How to Use Social Media, Blogs, News Releases, Online Video & Viral Marketing to Reach Buyers Directly*. Wiley (6th edition). 2017

Spence (Jr.), Roy M. *It's Not What You Sell, It's What You Stand For: Why Every Extraordinary Business Is Driven by Purpose*. Portfolio, 2011

Ziglar, Zig. *Ziglar on Selling*. Thomas Nelson, 2010

About the Author

Lauren Sapala is the author of *The INFJ Writer*, *Firefly Magic: Heart Powered Marketing for Highly Sensitive Writers*, and *The INFJ Revolution*, as well as *The West Coast Trilogy*, an autobiographical fiction series. She is also a writing coach for writers of the INFJ and INFP personality type and she blogs about writing, creativity, and personality theory at laurensapala.com.